GNU SASL

Simple Authentication and Security Layer for the GNU system
for version 1.8.0, 22 May 2012

Simon Josefsson

This manual was last updated 22 May 2012 for version 1.8.0 of GNU SASL.

Table of Contents

1 Introduction

This manual can be used in several ways. If read from the beginning to the end, it gives the reader an understanding of the SASL framework and the GNU SASL implementation, and how the GNU SASL library is used in an application. Forward references are included where necessary. Later on, the manual can be used as a reference manual to get just the information needed about any particular interface of the library. Experienced programmers might want to start looking at the examples at the end of the manual, and then only read up those parts of the interface which are unclear.

1.1 SASL Overview

SASL is a framework for application protocols, such as SMTP or IMAP, to add authentication support. For example, SASL is used to prove to the server who you are when you access an IMAP server to read your e-mail.

The SASL framework does not specify the technology used to perform the authentication, that is the responsibility for each SASL mechanism. Popular SASL mechanisms include CRAM-MD5 and GSSAPI (for Kerberos V5).

Typically a SASL negotiation works as follows. First the client requests authentication (possibly implicitly by connecting to the server). The server responds with a list of supported mechanisms. The client chose one of the mechanisms. The client and server then exchange data, one round-trip at a time, until authentication either succeeds or fails. After that, the client and server knows more about who is on the other end of the channel.

For example, in SMTP communication happens like this:

```
250-mail.example.com Hello pc.example.org [192.168.1.42], pleased to meet you
250-AUTH DIGEST-MD5 CRAM-MD5 LOGIN PLAIN
250 HELP
AUTH CRAM-MD5
334 PDk5MDgwNDEzMDUwNTUyMTE1NDQ5LjBAbG9jYWxob3N0Pg==
amFzIDBkZDRkODZkMDVjNjI4ODRkYzc3TcwODE4ZGI5MGY3
235 2.0.0 OK Authenticated
```

Here the first three lines are sent by the server and contains the list of supported mechanisms (DIGEST-MD5, CRAM-MD5, etc). The next line is sent by the client to select the CRAM-MD5 mechanism. The server replies with a challenge, which is a message that can be generated by calling GNU SASL functions. The client replies with a response, which also is a message that can be generated by GNU SASL functions. Depending on the mechanism, there can be more than one round trip, so do not assume all authentication exchanges consists of one message from the server and one from the client. The server accepts the authentication. At that point it knows it is talking to a authenticated client, and the application protocol can continue.

Essentially, your application is responsible for implementing the framing protocol (e.g., SMTP or XMPP) according to the particular specifications. Your application uses GNU SASL to generate the authentication messages.

1.2 Implementation

GNU SASL is an implementation of the Simple Authentication and Security Layer framework and a few common SASL mechanisms.

GNU SASL consists of a library (`libgsasl`), a command line utility (`gsasl`) to access the library from the shell, and a manual. The library includes support for the framework (with authentication functions and application data privacy and integrity functions) and at least partial support for the ANONYMOUS, CRAM-MD5, DIGEST-MD5, EXTERNAL, GS2-KRB5, GSSAPI, LOGIN, NTLM, PLAIN, SCRAM-SHA-1, SCRAM-SHA-1-PLUS, SAML20, OPENID20, and SECURID mechanisms.

The library is easily ported because it does not do network communication by itself, but rather leaves it up to the calling application. The library is flexible with regards to the authorization infrastructure used, as it utilizes a callback into the application to decide whether a user is authorized or not.

GNU SASL is developed for the GNU/Linux system, but runs on over 20 platforms including most major Unix platforms and Windows, and many kind of devices including iPAQ handhelds and S/390 mainframes.

GNU SASL is written in pure ANSI C89 to be portable to embedded and otherwise limited platforms. The entire library, with full support for ANONYMOUS, EXTERNAL, PLAIN, LOGIN and CRAM-MD5, and the front-end that supports client and server mode, and the IMAP and SMTP protocols, fits in under 80kb on an Intel x86 platform, without any modifications to the code. (This figure was accurate as of version 1.1.)

The design of the library and the intended interaction between applications and the library through the official API is illustrated below.

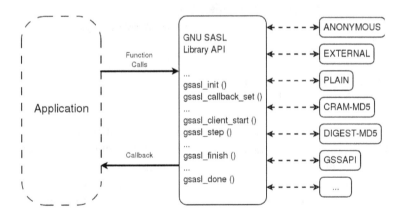

Illustration 1.1: Logical overview showing how applications use authentication mechanisms through an abstract interface.

1.3 Features

GNU SASL might have a couple of advantages over other libraries doing a similar job.

It's Free Software

> Anybody can use, modify, and redistribute it under the terms of the GNU General Public License version 3.0 or later. The library uses the GNU Lesser General Public License version 2.1 or later.

It's thread-safe
> No global variables are used and multiple library handles and session handles may be used in parallel.

It's internationalized
> It handles non-ASCII usernames and passwords and user visible strings used in the library (error messages) can be translated into the users' language.

It's portable
> It should work on all Unix like operating systems, including Windows. The library itself should be portable to any C89 system, not even POSIX is required.

It's small   The library has been rewritten with embedded platforms in mind. For example, no API consumes more than around 250 bytes of stack space.

Note that the library does not implement any policy to decide whether a certain user is "authenticated" or "authorized" or not. Rather, it uses a callback into the application to answer these questions.

1.4 Requirements

The GNU SASL library does not have any required external dependencies, but some optional features are enabled if you have a specific external library.

LibNTLM   The NTLM mechanism requires the library LibNTLM, http://www.nongnu.org/libntlm/.

GSS-API   The GSSAPI and GS2-KRB5 mechanisms requires a GSS-API library, see GNU GSS (http://www.gnu.org/software/gss/). MIT Kerberos or Heimdal are also supported.

LibIDN   Processing of non-ASCII usernames and passwords requires the SASLprep implementation in LibIDN (http://www.gnu.org/software/libidn/). This is needed for full conformance with the latest SASL protocol drafts, but is optional in the library for improved portability.

Libgcrypt   The GNU SASL library ships with its own cryptographic implementation, but it can use the one in libgcrypt (http://www.gnupg.org/) instead, if it is available. This is typically useful for desktop machines which have libgcrypt installed.

The command-line interface to GNU SASL requires a POSIX or Windows platform for network connectivity. The command-line tool can make use of GnuTLS (http://www.gnutls.org/) to support the STARTTLS modes of IMAP and SMTP, but GnuTLS is not required.

Note that the library does not need a POSIX platform or network connectivity.

1.5 Supported Platforms

GNU SASL has at some point in time been tested on the following platforms. Daily online build reports are available at http://autobuild.josefsson.org/gsasl/.

1. Debian GNU/Linux 3.0 (Woody)

   GCC 2.95.4 and GNU Make. This is the main development platform. `alphaev67-unknown-linux-gnu`, `alphaev6-unknown-linux-gnu`, `arm-unknown-linux-gnu`,

> hppa-unknown-linux-gnu, hppa64-unknown-linux-gnu, i686-pc-linux-gnu, ia64-unknown-linux-gnu, m68k-unknown-linux-gnu, mips-unknown-linux-gnu, mipsel-unknown-linux-gnu, powerpc-unknown-linux-gnu, s390-ibm-linux-gnu, sparc-unknown-linux-gnu.

2. Debian GNU/Linux 2.1

   GCC 2.95.1 and GNU Make. `armv4l-unknown-linux-gnu`.

3. Tru64 UNIX

   Tru64 UNIX C compiler and Tru64 Make. `alphaev67-dec-osf5.1`, `alphaev68-dec-osf5.1`.

4. SuSE Linux 7.1

   GCC 2.96 and GNU Make. `alphaev6-unknown-linux-gnu`, `alphaev67-unknown-linux-gnu`.

5. SuSE Linux 7.2a

   GCC 3.0 and GNU Make. `ia64-unknown-linux-gnu`.

6. RedHat Linux 7.2

   GCC 2.96 and GNU Make. `alphaev6-unknown-linux-gnu`, `alphaev67-unknown-linux-gnu`, `ia64-unknown-linux-gnu`.

7. RedHat Linux 8.0

   GCC 3.2 and GNU Make. `i686-pc-linux-gnu`.

8. RedHat Advanced Server 2.1

   GCC 2.96 and GNU Make. `i686-pc-linux-gnu`.

9. Slackware Linux 8.0.01

   GCC 2.95.3 and GNU Make. `i686-pc-linux-gnu`.

10. Mandrake Linux 9.0

    GCC 3.2 and GNU Make. `i686-pc-linux-gnu`.

11. IRIX 6.5

    MIPS C compiler, IRIX Make. `mips-sgi-irix6.5`.

12. AIX 4.3.2

    IBM C for AIX compiler, AIX Make. `rs6000-ibm-aix4.3.2.0`.

13. Microsoft Windows 2000 (Cygwin)

    GCC 3.2, GNU make. `i686-pc-cygwin`.

14. HP-UX 11

    HP-UX C compiler and HP Make. `ia64-hp-hpux11.22`, `hppa2.0w-hp-hpux11.11`.

15. SUN Solaris 2.8

    Sun WorkShop Compiler C 6.0 and SUN Make. `sparc-sun-solaris2.8`.

16. SUN Solaris 2.9

    Sun Forte Developer 7 C compiler and GNU Make. `sparc-sun-solaris2.9`.

17. NetBSD 1.6

    GCC 2.95.3 and GNU Make. `alpha-unknown-netbsd1.6`, `i386-unknown-netbsdelf1.6`.

18. OpenBSD 3.1 and 3.2

    GCC 2.95.3 and GNU Make. `alpha-unknown-openbsd3.1`, `i386-unknown-openbsd3.1`.

19. FreeBSD 4.7

    GCC 2.95.4 and GNU Make. `alpha-unknown-freebsd4.7`, `i386-unknown-freebsd4.7`.

20. Cross compiled to uClinux/uClibc on Motorola Coldfire.

    GCC 3.4 and GNU Make `m68k-uclinux-elf`.

If you port GNU SASL to a new platform, please report it to the author so this list can be updated.

1.6 Getting help

A mailing list where users may help each other exists, and you can reach it by sending e-mail to `help-gsasl@gnu.org`. Archives of the mailing list discussions, and an interface to manage subscriptions, is available through the World Wide Web at `http://lists.gnu.org/mailman/listinfo/help-gsasl/`.

1.7 Commercial Support

Commercial support is available for users of GNU SASL. The kind of support that can be purchased may include:

- Implement new features. Such as a new SASL mechanism.
- Port GNU SASL to new platforms. This could include porting to an embedded platforms that may need memory or size optimization.
- Integrating SASL as a security environment in your existing project.
- System design of components related to SASL.

If you are interested, please write to:

```
Simon Josefsson Datakonsult AB
Hagagatan 24
113 47 Stockholm
Sweden

E-mail: simon@josefsson.org
```

If your company provides support related to GNU SASL and would like to be mentioned here, contact the author (see Section 1.9 [Bug Reports], page 8).

1.8 Downloading and Installing

The package can be downloaded from several places, including:

`ftp://ftp.gnu.org/gnu/gsasl/`

The latest version is stored in a file, e.g., '`gsasl-1.8.0.tar.gz`' where the '`1.8.0`' value is the highest version number in the directory.

The package is then extracted, configured and built like many other packages that use Autoconf. For detailed information on configuring and building it, refer to the 'INSTALL' file that is part of the distribution archive.

Here is an example terminal session that downloads, configures, builds and install the package. You will need a few basic tools, such as 'sh', 'make' and 'cc'.

```
$ wget -q ftp://ftp.gnu.org/gnu/gsasl/gsasl-1.8.0.tar.gz
$ tar xfz gsasl-1.8.0.tar.gz
$ cd gsasl-1.8.0/
$ ./configure
...
$ make
...
$ make install
...
```

After that gsasl should be properly installed and ready for use.

A few **configure** options may be relevant, summarized in the table.

`--disable-client`
`--disable-server`

> If your target system require a minimal implementation, you may wish to disable the client or the server part of the code. This does not remove symbols from the library, so if you attempt to call an application that uses server functions in a library built with `--disable-server`, the function will return an error code.

`--disable-obsolete`

> Remove backwards compatibility (see Appendix B [Old Functions], page 75). Use if you want to limit the size of the library.

`--disable-anonymous`
`--disable-external`
`--disable-plain`
`--disable-login`
`--disable-securid`
`--disable-ntlm`
`--disable-cram-md5`
`--disable-digest-md5`
`--disable-gssapi`
`--disable-gs2`
`--enable-kerberos_v5`
`--disable-scram-sha1`
`--disable-saml20`
`--disable-openid20`

> Disable or enable individual mechanisms (see Chapter 5 [Mechanisms], page 26).

`--without-stringprep`

> Disable internationalized string processing. Note that this will result in a SASL library that is only compatible with RFC 2222.

For the complete list, refer to the output from **configure --help**.

1.8.1 Installing under Windows

There are two ways to build GNU SASL on Windows: via MinGW or via Microsoft Visual Studio. Note that a binary release for Windows is available from `http://josefsson.org/gnutls4win/`.

With MinGW, you can build a GNU SASL DLL and use it from other applications. After installing MinGW (`http://mingw.org/`) follow the generic installation instructions (see Section 1.8 [Downloading and Installing], page 5). The DLL is installed by default.

For information on how to use the DLL in other applications, see: `http://www.mingw.org/mingwfaq.shtml#faq-msvcdll`.

You can build GNU SASL as a native Visual Studio C++ project. This allows you to build the code for other platforms that VS supports, such as Windows Mobile. You need Visual Studio 2005 or later.

First download and unpack the archive as described in the generic installation instructions (see Section 1.8 [Downloading and Installing], page 5). Don't run `./configure`. Instead, start Visual Studio and open the project file 'lib/win32/libgsasl.sln' inside the GNU SASL directory. You should be able to build the project using Build Project.

Output libraries will be written into the `lib/win32/lib` (or `lib/win32/lib/debug` for Debug versions) folder.

Warning! Unless you build GNU SASL linked with libgcrypt, GNU SASL uses the Windows function `CryptGenRandom` for generating cryptographic random data. The function is known to have some security weaknesses. See `http://eprint.iacr.org/2007/419` for more information. The code will attempt to use the Intel RND crypto provider if it is installed, see 'lib/gl/gc-gnulib.c'.

1.8.2 Kerberos on Windows

Building GNU SASL with support for Kerberos via GSS-API on Windows is straight forward if you use GNU GSS and GNU Shishi as the Kerberos implementation.

If you are using MIT Kerberos for Windows (KfW), getting GNU SASL to build with Kerberos support is not straightforward because KfW does not follow the GNU coding style and it has bugs that needs to be worked around. We provide instructions for this environment as well, in the hope that it will be useful for GNU SASL users.

Our instructions assumes you are building the software on a dpkg-based GNU/Linux systems (e.g., gNewSense) using the MinGW cross-compiler suite. These instructions were compiled for KfW version 3.2.2 which were the latest as of 2010-09-25.

We assume that you have installed a normal build environment including the MinGW cross-compiler. Download and unpack the KfW SDK like this:

```
$ mkdir ~/kfw
$ cd ~/kfw
$ wget -q http://web.mit.edu/kerberos/dist/kfw/3.2/kfw-3.2.2/kfw-3-2-2-sdk.zip
$ unzip kfw-3-2-2-sdk.zip
```

Fix a bug in the "win-mac.h" header inside KfW by replacing #include <sys\foo.h> with #include <sys/foo.h>:

```
perl -pi -e 's,sys\\,sys/,' ~/kfw/kfw-3-2-2-final/inc/krb5/win-mac.h
```

Unpack your copy of GNU SASL:

```
$ wget -q ftp://alpha.gnu.org/gnu/gsasl/gsasl-1.8.0.tar.gz
$ tar xfz gsasl-1.8.0.tar.gz
$ cd gsasl-1.8.0
```

Configure GNU SASL like this:

```
$ lt_cv_deplibs_check_method=pass_all ./configure --host=i586-mingw32msvc --build=
```

The 'lt_cv_deplibs_check_method=pass_all' setting is required because the KfW SDK does not ship with Libtool *.la files and is using non-standard DLL names. The -DSSIZE_T_DEFINED is necessary because the win-mac.h file would provide an incorrect duplicate definitions of ssize_t otherwise. By passing --with-gssapi-impl=kfw you activate other bug workarounds, such as providing a GSS_C_NT_HOSTBASED_SERVICE symbol.

Build the software using:

```
$ make
```

If you have Wine installed and your kernel is able to invoke it automatically for Windows programs, you can run the self tests. This is recommended to make sure the build is sane.

```
$ make check
```

You may get error messages about missing DLLs, like this error:

```
err:module:import_dll Library gssapi32.dll (which is needed by L"Z:\\home\\jas\\sr
```

If that happens, you need to make sure that Wine can find the appropriate DLL. The simplest solution is to copy the necessary DLLs to ~/.wine/drive_c/windows/system32/.

You may now copy the following files onto the Windows machine (e.g., through a USB memory device):

```
lib/src/.libs/libgsasl-7.dll
src/.libs/gsasl.exe
```

The remaining steps are done on the Windows XP machine. Install KfW and configure it for your realm. To make sure KfW is working properly, acquire a user ticket and then remove it. For testing purposes, you may use the realm 'interop.josefsson.org' with KDC 'interop.josefsson.org' and username 'user' and password 'pass'.

Change to the directory where you placed the files above, and invoke a command like this:

```
gsasl.exe -d interop.josefsson.org
```

KfW should query you for a password, and the tool should negotiate authentication against the server using GS2-KRB5.

1.9 Bug Reports

If you think you have found a bug in GNU SASL, please investigate it and report it.

- Please make sure that the bug is really in GNU SASL, and preferably also check that it hasn't already been fixed in the latest version.

- You have to send us a test case that makes it possible for us to reproduce the bug.

- You also have to explain what is wrong; if you get a crash, or if the results printed are not good and in that case, in what way. Make sure that the bug report includes all information you would need to fix this kind of bug for someone else.

Please make an effort to produce a self-contained report, with something definite that can be tested or debugged. Vague queries or piecemeal messages are difficult to act on and don't help the development effort.

If your bug report is good, we will do our best to help you to get a corrected version of the software; if the bug report is poor, we won't do anything about it (apart from asking you to send better bug reports).

If you think something in this manual is unclear, or downright incorrect, or if the language needs to be improved, please also send a note.

Send your bug report to:

'bug-gsasl@gnu.org'

1.10 Contributing

If you want to submit a patch for inclusion – from solve a typo you discovered, up to adding support for a new feature – you should submit it as a bug report (see Section 1.9 [Bug Reports], page 8). There are some things that you can do to increase the chances for it to be included in the official package.

Unless your patch is very small (say, under 10 lines) we require that you assign the copyright of your work to the Free Software Foundation. This is to protect the freedom of the project. If you have not already signed papers, we will send you the necessary information when you submit your contribution.

For contributions that doesn't consist of actual programming code, the only guidelines are common sense. Use it.

For code contributions, a number of style guides will help you:

- Coding Style. Follow the GNU Standards document (see ⟨undefined⟩ [top], page ⟨undefined⟩).

  If you normally code using another coding standard, there is no problem, but you should use 'indent' to reformat the code (see ⟨undefined⟩ [top], page ⟨undefined⟩) before submitting your work.

- Use the unified diff format 'diff -u'.

- Return errors. No reason whatsoever should abort the execution of the library. Even memory allocation errors, e.g. when malloc return NULL, should work although result in an error code.

- Design with thread safety in mind. Don't use global variables. Don't even write to per-handle global variables unless the documented behaviour of the function you write is to write to the per-handle global variable.

- Avoid using the C math library. It causes problems for embedded implementations, and in most situations it is very easy to avoid using it.

- Document your functions. Use comments before each function headers, that, if properly formatted, are extracted into Texinfo manuals and GTK-DOC web pages.

- Supply a ChangeLog and NEWS entries, where appropriate.

2 Preparation

To use GNU SASL, you have to perform some changes to your sources and the build system. The necessary changes are small and explained in the following sections. At the end of this chapter, it is described how the library is initialized, and how the requirements of the library are verified.

A faster way to find out how to adapt your application for use with GNU SASL may be to look at the examples at the end of this manual (see Chapter 13 [Examples], page 51).

2.1 Header

All interfaces (data types and functions) of the library are defined in the header file `gsasl.h`. You must include this in all programs using the library, either directly or through some other header file, like this:

```
#include <gsasl.h>
```

The name space is `gsasl_*` for function names, `Gsasl*` for data types and `GSASL_*` for other symbols. In addition the same name prefixes with one prepended underscore are reserved for internal use and should never be used by an application.

2.2 Initialization

The library must be initialized before it can be used. The library is initialized by calling `gsasl_init` (see Chapter 6 [Global Functions], page 33). The resources allocated by the initialization process can be released if the application no longer has a need to call 'Libgsasl' functions, this is done by calling `gsasl_done`. For example:

```
int
main (int argc, char *argv[])
{
  Gsasl *ctx = NULL;
  int rc;
...
  rc = gsasl_init (&ctx);
  if (rc != GSASL_OK)
    {
      printf ("SASL initialization failure (%d): %s\n",
              rc, gsasl_strerror (rc));
      return 1;
    }
  ...
```

In order to make error messages from `gsasl_strerror` be translated (see Section "Top" in *GNU Gettext*) the application must set the current locale using `setlocale` before calling `gsasl_init`. For example:

```
int
main (int argc, char *argv[])
{
  Gsasl *ctx = NULL;
```

```
    int rc;
...
    setlocale (LC_ALL, "");
...
  rc = gsasl_init (&ctx);
  if (rc != GSASL_OK)
    {
      printf (gettext ("SASL initialization failure (%d): %s\n"),
              rc, gsasl_strerror (rc));
      return 1;
    }
...
```

In order to take advantage of the secure memory features in Libgcrypt[1], you need to initialize secure memory in your application, and for some platforms even make your application setuid root. See the Libgcrypt documentation for more information. Here is example code to initialize secure memory in your code:

```
#include <gcrypt.h>
...
int
main (int argc, char *argv[])
{
  Gsasl *ctx = NULL;
  int rc;
...
  /* Check version of libgcrypt. */
  if (!gcry_check_version (GCRYPT_VERSION))
    die ("version mismatch\n");

  /* Allocate a pool of 16k secure memory.  This also drops priviliges
     on some systems. */
  gcry_control (GCRYCTL_INIT_SECMEM, 16384, 0);

  /* Tell Libgcrypt that initialization has completed. */
  gcry_control (GCRYCTL_INITIALIZATION_FINISHED, 0);
...
  rc = gsasl_init (&ctx);
  if (rc != GSASL_OK)
    {
      printf ("SASL initialization failure (%d): %s\n",
              rc, gsasl_strerror (rc));
      return 1;
    }
...
```

---

[1] Note that GNU SASL normally use its own internal implementation of the cryptographic functions. Take care to verify that GNU SASL really use Libgcrypt, if this is what you want.

If you do not do this, keying material will not be allocated in secure memory (which, for most applications, is not the biggest secure problem anyway). Note that the GNU SASL Library has not been audited to make sure it stores passwords or keys in secure memory.

2.3 Version Check

It is often desirable to check that the version of the library used is indeed one which fits all requirements. Even with binary compatibility, new features may have been introduced but, due to problem with the dynamic linker, an old version may actually be used. So you may want to check that the version is okay right after program startup.

gsasl_check_version

const char * gsasl_check_version (*const char * req_version*)   [Function]
    req_version: version string to compare with, or NULL.

    Check GNU SASL Library version.

    See GSASL_VERSION for a suitable req_version string.

    This function is one of few in the library that can be used without a successful call to gsasl_init().

    Return value: Check that the version of the library is at minimum the one given as a string in req_version and return the actual version string of the library; return NULL if the condition is not met. If NULL is passed to this function no check is done and only the version string is returned.

The normal way to use the function is to put something similar to the following early in your main:

```
if (!gsasl_check_version (GSASL_VERSION))
  {
    printf ("gsasl_check_version failed:\n"
            "Header file incompatible with shared library.\n");
    exit(1);
  }
```

2.4 Building the source

If you want to compile a source file including the 'gsasl.h' header file, you must make sure that the compiler can find it in the directory hierarchy. This is accomplished by adding the path to the directory in which the header file is located to the compilers include file search path (via the '-I' option).

However, the path to the include file is determined at the time the source is configured. To solve this problem, the library uses the external package pkg-config that knows the path to the include file and other configuration options. The options that need to be added to the compiler invocation at compile time are output by the '--cflags' option to pkg-config libgsasl. The following example shows how it can be used at the command line:

```
gcc -c foo.c `pkg-config libgsasl --cflags`
```

Adding the output of 'pkg-config libgsasl --cflags' to the compiler command line will ensure that the compiler can find the 'gsasl.h' header file.

A similar problem occurs when linking the program with the library. Again, the compiler
has to find the library files. For this to work, the path to the library files has to be added to
the library search path (via the '-L' option). For this, the option '--libs' to pkg-config
libgsasl can be used. For convenience, this option also outputs all other options that
are required to link the program with the library (for instance, the '-lidn' option). The
example shows how to link 'foo.o' with the library to a program foo.

```
gcc -o foo foo.o `pkg-config libgsasl --libs`
```

Of course you can also combine both examples to a single command by specifying both
options to pkg-config:

```
gcc -o foo foo.c `pkg-config libgsasl --cflags --libs`
```

2.5 Autoconf tests

If you work on a project that uses Autoconf (see ⟨undefined⟩ [top], page ⟨undefined⟩) to help
find installed libraries, the suggestions in the previous section are not the entire story. There
are a few methods to detect and incorporate the GNU SASL Library into your Autoconf
based package. The preferred approach, is to use Libtool in your project, and use the
normal Autoconf header file and library tests.

2.5.1 Autoconf test via 'pkg-config'

If your audience is a typical GNU/Linux desktop, you can often assume they have the
'pkg-config' tool installed, in which you can use its Autoconf M4 macro to find and set
up your package for use with Libgsasl. The following example illustrates this scenario.

```
AC_ARG_ENABLE(gsasl,
  AC_HELP_STRING([--disable-gsasl], [don't use GNU SASL]),
  gsasl=$enableval)
if test "$gsasl" != "no" ; then
  PKG_CHECK_MODULES(GSASL, libgsasl >= 1.8.0,
    [gsasl=yes],
    [gsasl=no])
  if test "$gsasl" != "yes" ; then
    gsasl=no
    AC_MSG_WARN([Cannot find GNU SASL, disabling])
  else
    gsasl=yes
    AC_DEFINE(USE_GSASL, 1, [Define to 1 if you want GNU SASL.])
  fi
fi
AC_MSG_CHECKING([if GNU SASL should be used])
AC_MSG_RESULT($gsasl)
```

2.5.2 Standalone Autoconf test using Libtool

If your package uses Libtool (see ⟨undefined⟩ [top], page ⟨undefined⟩), you can use the
normal Autoconf tests to find Libgsasl and rely on the Libtool dependency tracking to
include the proper dependency libraries (e.g., Libidn). The following example illustrates
this scenario.

```
AC_CHECK_HEADER(gsasl.h,
  AC_CHECK_LIB(gsasl, gsasl_check_version,
    [gsasl=yes AC_SUBST(GSASL_LIBS, -lgsasl)],
    gsasl=no),
  gsasl=no)
AC_ARG_ENABLE(gsasl,
  AC_HELP_STRING([--disable-gsasl], [don't use GNU SASL]),
  gsasl=$enableval)
if test "$gsasl" != "no" ; then
  AC_DEFINE(USE_SASL, 1, [Define to 1 if you want GNU SASL.])
else
  AC_MSG_WARN([Cannot find GNU SASL, diabling])
fi
AC_MSG_CHECKING([if GNU SASL should be used])
AC_MSG_RESULT($gsasl)
```

3 Using the Library

Your application's use of the library can be roughly modeled into the following steps: initialize the library, optionally specify the callback, perform the authentication, and finally clean up. The following image illustrates this.

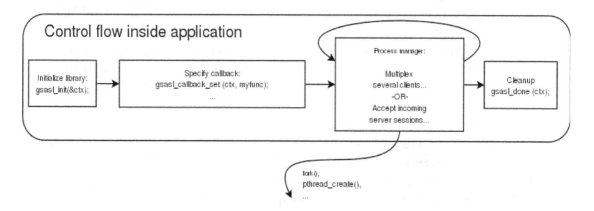

The third step may look complex, but for a simple client it will actually not involve any code. If your application needs to handle several concurrent clients, or if it is a server that needs to serve many clients simultaneous, things do get a bit more complicated.

For illustration, we will write a simple client. Writing a server would be similar, the only difference is that, later on, instead of supplying a username and password, you need to decide whether someone should be allowed to log in or not. The code for what we have discussed so far make up the **main** function in our client (see Section 13.1 [Example 1], page 51):

```
int main (int argc, char *argv[])
{
  Gsasl *ctx = NULL;
  int rc;

  if ((rc = gsasl_init (&ctx)) != GSASL_OK)
    {
      printf ("Cannot initialize libgsasl (%d): %s",
              rc, gsasl_strerror (rc));
      return 1;
    }

  client (ctx);

  gsasl_done (ctx);

  return 0;
}
```

Here, the call to the function **client** correspond to the third step in the image above.

For a more complicated application, having several clients running simultaneous, instead of a simple call to `client`, it may have created new threads for each session, and call `client` within each thread. The library is thread safe.

An actual authentication session is more complicated than what we have seen so far. These are the steps: decide which mechanism to use, start the session, optionally specify the callback, optionally set any properties, perform the authentication loop, and clean up. Naturally, your application will start to talk its own protocol (e.g., SMTP or IMAP) after these steps have concluded.

The authentication loop is based on sending tokens (typically short messages encoded in base 64) back and forth between the client and server. It continues until authentication succeeds or an error occurs. The format of the data to be transferred, the number of iterations in the loop, and other details are specified by each mechanism. The goal of the library is to isolate your application from the details of all different mechanisms.

Note that the library does not send data to the server itself, but returns it in an buffer. You must send it to the server, following an application protocol profile. For example, the SASL application protocol profile for SMTP is described in RFC 2554.

The following image illustrates the steps we have been talking about.

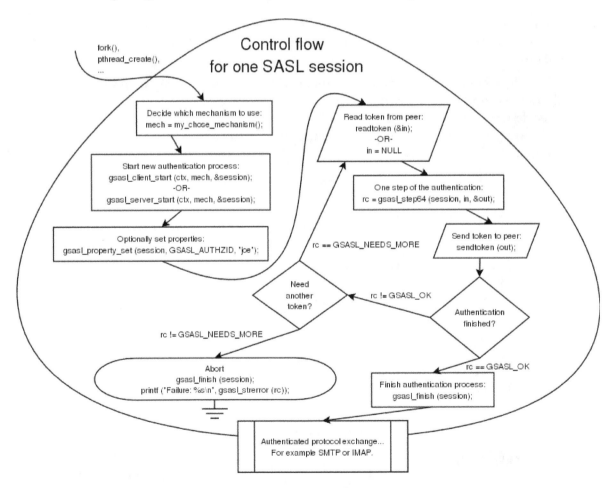

We will now show the implementation of the `client` function used before.

```
void client (Gsasl *ctx)
{
  Gsasl_session *session;
  const char *mech = "PLAIN";
  int rc;

  /* Create new authentication session. */
  if ((rc = gsasl_client_start (ctx, mech, &session)) != GSASL_OK)
    {
      printf ("Cannot initialize client (%d): %s\n",
              rc, gsasl_strerror (rc));
      return;
    }

  /* Set username and password in session handle.  This info will be
     lost when this session is deallocated below.  */
  gsasl_property_set (session, GSASL_AUTHID, "jas");
  gsasl_property_set (session, GSASL_PASSWORD, "secret");

  /* Do it. */
  client_authenticate (session);

  /* Cleanup. */
  gsasl_finish (session);
}
```

This function is responsible for deciding which mechanism to use. In this case, the
'PLAIN' mechanism is hard coded, but you will see later how this can be made more flexible.
The function creates a new session, then it stores the username and password in the session
handle, then it calls another function client_authenticate to handle the authentication
loop, and finally it cleans up up. Let's continue with the implementation of client_
authenticate.

```
void client_authenticate (Gsasl_session * session)
{
  char buf[BUFSIZ] = "";
  char *p;
  int rc;

  /* This loop mimics a protocol where the server sends data
     first. */

  do
    {
      printf ("Input base64 encoded data from server:\n");
      fgets (buf, sizeof (buf) - 1, stdin);
      if (buf[strlen (buf) - 1] == '\n')
        buf[strlen (buf) - 1] = '\0';
```

```
        rc = gsasl_step64 (session, buf, &p);

        if (rc == GSASL_NEEDS_MORE || rc == GSASL_OK)
          {
            printf ("Output:\n%s\n", p);
            free (p);
          }
      }
    while (rc == GSASL_NEEDS_MORE);

    printf ("\n");

    if (rc != GSASL_OK)
      {
        printf ("Authentication error (%d): %s\n",
                rc, gsasl_strerror (rc));
        return;
      }

    /* The client is done.  Here you would typically check if the
       server let the client in.  If not, you could try again. */

    printf ("If server accepted us, we're done.\n");
  }
```

This last function needs to be discussed in some detail. First, you should be aware that there are two versions of this function, that differ in a subtle way. The version above (see Section 13.2 [Example 2], page 53) is used for application profiles where the server sends data first. For some mechanisms, this may waste a roundtrip, because the server needs input from the client to proceed. Therefor, today the recommended approach is to permit client to send data first (see Section 13.1 [Example 1], page 51). Which version you should use depends on which application protocol you are implementing.

Further, you should realize that it is bad programming style to use a fixed size buffer. On GNU systems, you may use the `getline` functions instead of `fgets`. However, in practice, there are few mechanisms that use very large tokens. In typical configurations, the mechanism with the largest tokens (GSSAPI) can use at least 500 bytes. A fixed buffer size of 8192 bytes may thus be sufficient for now. But don't say I didn't warn you, when a future mechanism doesn't work in your application, because of a fixed size buffer.

The function `gsasl_step64` (and of course also `gasl_step`) returns two non-error return codes. `GSASL_OK` is used for success, indicating that the library considers the authentication finished. That may include a successful server authentication, depending on the mechanism. You must not let the client continue to the application protocol part unless you receive `GSASL_OK` from these functions. In particular, don't be fooled into believing authentication were successful if the server replies "OK" but these functions have failed with an error. The server may have been hacked, and could be tricking you into sending confidential data, without having successfully authenticated the server.

The non-error return code `GSASL_NEEDS_MORE` is used to signal to your application that you should send the output token to the peer, and wait for a new token, and do another iteration. If the server concludes the authentication process, with no data, you should call `gsasl_step64` (or `gsasl_step`) specifying a zero-length token.

If the functions (`gsasl_step` and `gsasl_step64`) return any non-error code, the content of the output buffer is undefined. Otherwise, it is the callers responsibility to deallocate the buffer, by calling `free`. Note that in some situations, where the buffer is empty, `NULL` is returned as the buffer value. You should treat this as an empty buffer.

3.1 Choosing a mechanism

Our earlier code was hard coded to use a specific mechanism. This is rarely a good idea. Instead, it is recommended to select the best mechanism available from the list of mechanisms supported by the server. Note that without TLS or similar, the list may have been maliciously altered, by an attacker. This means that you should abort if you cannot find any mechanism that exceeds your minimum security level. There is a function `gsasl_client_suggest_mechanism` (see Chapter 6 [Global Functions], page 33) that will try to pick the "best" available mechanism from a list of mechanisms. Our simple interactive example client (see Section 13.3 [Example 3], page 56) includes the following function to decide which mechanism to use. Note that the code doesn't blindly use what is returned from `gsasl_client_suggest_mechanism`, rather it lets some logic (in this case the user, through an interactive query) decide which mechanism is acceptable.

```
const char *client_mechanism (Gsasl *ctx)
{
  static char mech[GSASL_MAX_MECHANISM_SIZE + 1] = "";
  char mechlist[BUFSIZ] = "";
  const char *suggestion;

  printf ("Enter list of server supported mechanisms, separate by SPC:\n");
  fgets (mechlist, sizeof (mechlist) - 1, stdin);

  suggestion = gsasl_client_suggest_mechanism (ctx, mechlist);
  if (suggestion)
    printf ("Library suggests use of '%s'.\n", suggestion);

  printf ("Enter mechanism to use:\n");
  fgets (mech, sizeof (mech) - 1, stdin);
  mech[strlen (mech) - 1] = '\0';

  return mech;
}
```

When running this example code, it might look like in the following output.

```
Enter list server supported mechanisms, separate by SPC:
CRAM-MD5 DIGEST-MD5 GSSAPI FOO BAR
Library suggests use of 'GSSAPI'.
Enter mechanism to use:
```

```
CRAM-MD5
Input base64 encoded data from server:
Zm5vcmQ=
Output:
amFzIDkyY2U1NWE5MTM2ZTY4NzEyMTUyZTFjYmFmNjVkZjgx
```

```
If server accepted us, we're done.
```

3.2 Using a callback

Our earlier code specified the username and password before the authentication loop, as in:

```
gsasl_property_set (ctx, GSASL_AUTHID, "jas");
gsasl_property_set (ctx, GSASL_PASSWORD, "secret");
```

This may work for simple mechanisms, that need only a username and a password. But some mechanism requires more information, such as an authorization identity, a special PIN or passcode, a realm, a hostname, a service name, or an anonymous identifier. Querying the user for all that information, without knowing exactly which of it is really needed will result in a poor user interface. The user should not have to input private information, if it isn't required.

The approach is a bad idea for another reason. What if the server aborts the authentication process? Then your application has already queried the user for a username and password. It would be better if you only asked the user for this information, annoying to input, when it is known to be needed.

A better approach to this problem is to use a callback. Then the mechanism may query your application whenever it needs some information, like the username and password. It will only do this at the precise step in the authentication when the information is actually needed. Further, if the user aborts, e.g., a password prompt, the mechanism is directly informed of this (because it invoked the callback), and could recover somehow.

Our final example (see Section 13.4 [Example 4], page 59) specifies a callback function, inside main as below.

```
/* Set the callback handler for the library. */
gsasl_callback_set (ctx, callback);
```

The function itself is implemented as follows.

```
int callback (Gsasl * ctx, Gsasl_session * sctx, Gsasl_property prop)
{
  char buf[BUFSIZ] = "";
  int rc = GSASL_NO_CALLBACK;

  /* Get user info from user. */

  printf ("Callback invoked, for property %d.\n", prop);

  switch (prop)
    {
    case GSASL_PASSCODE:
```

```
        printf ("Enter passcode:\n");
        fgets (buf, sizeof (buf) - 1, stdin);
        buf[strlen (buf) - 1] = '\0';

        gsasl_property_set (sctx, GSASL_PASSCODE, buf);
        rc = GSASL_OK;
        break;

      case GSASL_AUTHID:
        printf ("Enter username:\n");
        fgets (buf, sizeof (buf) - 1, stdin);
        buf[strlen (buf) - 1] = '\0';

        gsasl_property_set (sctx, GSASL_AUTHID, buf);
        rc = GSASL_OK;
        break;

      default:
        printf ("Unknown property!  Don't worry.\n");
        break;
      }

    return rc;
  }
```

Again, it is bad style to use a fixed size buffer. Mmm'kay.

Which properties you should handle is up to you. If you don't know how to respond to a certain property, simply return GSASL_NO_CALLBACK. The basic properties to support are authentication identity (GSASL_AUTHID), authorization identity (GSASL_AUTHZID), and password (GSASL_PASSWORD). See Chapter 4 [Properties], page 22, for the list of all properties, and what your callback should (ideally) do for them, and which properties each mechanism require in order to work.

4 Properties

The library uses a concept called "properties" to request and pass data between the application and the individual authentication mechanisms. The application can set property values using the `gsasl_property_set` function. If a mechanism needs a property value the application has not yet provided, this is handled through a callback. The application provides a callback, using `gsasl_callback_set`, which will be invoked with a property parameter. The callback should set the property before returning, or fail. See Chapter 7 [Callback Functions], page 35, for more information.

There are two kind of properties. The first, a "data property" is the simplest to understand because it normally refers to short strings. For example, the property called `GSASL_AUTHID` correspond to the username string, e.g., `simon`.

The latter properties, called "logical properties", are used by the server to make a authentication decision, and is used as a way to get the application callback invoked. For example, the property `GSASL_VALIDATE_SIMPLE` is used by the server-side part of mechanisms like `PLAIN`. The purpose is to ask the server application to decide whether the user should be authenticated successfully or not. The callback typically look at other property fields, such as `GSASL_AUTHID` and `GSASL_PASSWORD`, and compare those values with external information (for example data stored in a database or on a LDAP server) and then return OK or not.

> **Warning:** Don't expect that all mechanisms invoke one of the logical properties in the server mode. For example, the CRAM-MD5 and SCRAM-SHA-1 mechanisms will use the data properties (i.e., username and password) provided by the application to internally decide whether to successfully authenticate the user. User authorization decisions needs to be made by the application outside of the SASL mechanism negotiation.

The logical properties are currently only used by servers, but data properties are used by both client and servers. It makes sense to think about the latter category as '**server properties**' but the reverse is not valid nor useful.

The semantics associated with a data property is different when it is used in client context and in the server context. For example, in the client context, the application is expected to set the property `GSASL_AUTHID` to signal to the mechanism the username to use, but in the server context, the `GSASL_AUTHID` property is set by the mechanism and can be used by the application (in the callback) to find out what username the client provided.

Below is a list of all properties and an explanation for each. First is the list of data properties:

- `GSASL_AUTHID`

  The authentication identity.

- `GSASL_AUTHZID`

  The authorization identity.

- `GSASL_PASSWORD`

  The password of the authentication identity.

- `GSASL_ANONYMOUS_TOKEN`

  The anonymous token. This is typically the email address of the user.

- `GSASL_SERVICE`

  The registered GSSAPI service name of the application service, e.g. "imap". While the names are registered for GSSAPI, other mechanisms such as DIGEST-MD5 may also use this.

- `GSASL_HOSTNAME`

  Should be the local host name of the machine.

- `GSASL_GSSAPI_DISPLAY_NAME`

  Contain the GSSAPI "display name", set by the server GSSAPI mechanism. Typically you retrieve this property in your callback, when invoked for `GSASL_VALIDATE_GSSAPI`.

- `GSASL_REALM`

  The name of the authentication domain. This is used by several mechanisms, including DIGEST-MD5, GSS-API, KERBEROS_V5 and NTLM.

- `GSASL_PASSCODE`

  The SecurID passcode.

- `GSASL_PIN`

  The SecurID personal identification number (PIN).

- `GSASL_SUGGESTED_PIN`

  A SecurID personal identification number (PIN) suggested by the server.

- `GSASL_DIGEST_MD5_HASHED_PASSWORD`

  For the DIGEST-MD5 mechanism, this is a hashed password. It is used in servers to avoid storing clear-text credentials.

- `GSASL_QOPS`

  The DIGEST-MD5 server query for this property to get the set of quality of protection (QOP) values to advertise. The property holds strings with comma separated keywords denoting the set of qops to use, for example `qop-auth, qop-int`. Valid keywords are `qop-auth`, `qop-int`, and `qop-conf`.

- `GSASL_QOP`

  The DIGEST-MD5 client query for this property to get the quality of protection (QOP) values to request. The property value is one of the keywords for `GSASL_QOPS`. The client must chose one of the QOP values offered by the server (which may be inspected through the `GSASL_QOPS` property).

- `GSASL_SCRAM_SALTED_PASSWORD`

  The SCRAM-SHA-1 client requests this property from the application, and the value should be 40 character long hex-encoded string with the user's hashed password. Note that the value is different for the same password for each value of the `GSASL_SCRAM_ITER` and `GSASL_SCRAM_ITER` properties. The property can be used to avoid storing a clear-text credential in the client. If the property is not available, the client will ask for the `GSASL_PASSWORD` property instead.

- `GSASL_SCRAM_ITER`

- `GSASL_SCRAM_ITER`

  In the server, the application can set these properties to influence the hash iteration count and hash salt to use when deriving the password. The default hash iteration count is 4096 and normally you should not need to use a lower setting. The salt should be a random string. In the client, the SCRAM-SHA-1 mechanism set these properties before asking for asking the application to provide a `GSASL_SCRAM_SALTED_PASSWORD` value.

- `GSASL_CB_TLS_UNIQUE`

  This property holds base64 encoded `tls-unique` channel binding data. As a hint, if you use GnuTLS, the API `gnutls_session_channel_binding` can be used to extract channel bindings for a session.

- `GSASL_SAML20_IDP_IDENTIFIER`

  This property holds the SAML identifier of the user. The SAML20 mechanism in client mode will send it to the other end for identification purposes, and in server mode it will be accessible in the `GSASL_SAML20_REDIRECT_URL` callback.

- `GSASL_SAML20_REDIRECT_URL` This property holds the SAML redirect URL that the server wants the client to access. It will be available in the `GSASL_SAML20_AUTHENTICATE_IN_BROWSER` callback for the client.

- `GSASL_OPENID20_REDIRECT_URL` This property holds the SAML redirect URL that the server wants the client to access. It will be available in the `GSASL_OPENID20_AUTHENTICATE_IN_BROWSER` callback for the client.

- `GSASL_OPENID20_OUTCOME_DATA` OpenID 2.0 authentication outcome data. This is either the OpenID SREG values or a value list starting with `"openid.error="` to signal error.

Next follows a list of data properties used to trigger the callback, typically used in servers to validate client credentials:

- `GSASL_VALIDATE_SIMPLE`

  Used by multiple mechanisms in server mode. The callback may retrieve the `GSASL_AUTHID`, `GSASL_AUTHZID` and `GSASL_PASSWORD` property values and use them to make an authentication and authorization decision.

- `GSASL_VALIDATE_EXTERNAL`

  Used by EXTERNAL mechanism on the server side to validate the client. The GSASL_AUTHID will contain the authorization identity of the client.

- `GSASL_VALIDATE_ANONYMOUS`

  Used by ANONYMOUS mechanism on the server side to validate the client. The GSASL_ANONYMOUS_TOKEN will contain token that identity the client.

- `GSASL_VALIDATE_GSSAPI`

  Used by the GSSAPI and GS2-KRB5 mechanisms on the server side, to validate the client. You may retrieve the authorization identity from GSASL_AUTHZID and the GSS-API display name from GSASL_GSSAPI_DISPLAY_NAME.

- `GSASL_VALIDATE_SECURID`

  Used by SECURID mechanism on the server side to validate client. The GSASL_AUTHID, GSASL_AUTHZID, GSASL_PASSCODE, and GSASL_PIN will be set. It can return GSASL_SECURID_SERVER_NEED_ADDITIONAL_PASSCODE to ask the client to supply another passcode, and GSASL_SECURID_SERVER_NEED_NEW_PIN to require the client to supply a new PIN code.

- `GSASL_VALIDATE_SAML20`

  Used by the SAML20 mechanism on the server side to request that the application perform authentication. The callback should return `GSASL_OK` if the user should be permitted access, and `GSASL_AUTHENTICATION_ERROR` (or another error code) otherwise.

- `GSASL_VALIDATE_OPENID20`

  Used by the OPENID20 mechanism on the server side to request that the application perform authentication. The callback should return `GSASL_OK` if the user should be permitted access, and `GSASL_AUTHENTICATION_ERROR` (or another error code) otherwise.

- `GSASL_SAML20_AUTHENTICATE_IN_BROWSER` Used by the SAML20 mechanism in the client side to request that the client should launch the SAML redirect URL (the `GSASL_SAML20_REDIRECT_URL` property) in a browser to continue with authentication.

- `GSASL_OPENID20_AUTHENTICATE_IN_BROWSER` Used by the OPENID20 mechanism in the client side to request that the client should launch the OpenID redirect URL (the `GSASL_OPENID20_REDIRECT_URL` property) in a browser to continue with authentication.

5 Mechanisms

Different SASL mechanisms have different requirements on the application using it. To handle these differences the library can use a callback function into your application in several different ways. Some mechanisms, such as 'PLAIN', are simple to explain and use. The client callback queries the user for a username and password. The server callback hands the username and password into any local policy deciding authentication system (such as '/etc/passwd' via PAM).

Mechanism such as 'CRAM-MD5' and 'SCRAM-SHA-1' uses hashed passwords. The client callback behaviour is the same as for PLAIN. However, the server does not receive the plain text password over the network but rather a hash of it. Existing policy deciding systems like PAM cannot handle this, so the server callback for these mechanisms are more complicated.

Further, mechanisms like GSSAPI/GS2-KRB5 (Kerberos 5) assume a specific authentication system. In theory this means that the SASL library would not need to interact with the application, but rather call this specific authentication system directly. However, some callbacks are supported anyway, to modify the behaviour of how the specific authentication system is used (i.e., to handle "super-user" login as some other user).

Some mechanisms, like 'EXTERNAL' and 'ANONYMOUS' are entirely dependent on callbacks.

5.1 The EXTERNAL mechanism

The EXTERNAL mechanism is used to authenticate a user to a server based on out-of-band authentication. EXTERNAL is typically used over TLS authenticated channels. Note that in the server, you need to make sure that TLS actually authenticated the client successfully. It is normally not sufficient to use TLS, since it also supports anonymous modes.

In the client, this mechanism is always enabled, and it will send the GSASL_AUTHZID property as the authorization name to the server, if the property is set. If the property is not set, the empty authorization name is sent. You need not implement a callback.

In the server, this mechanism will request the GSASL_VALIDATE_EXTERNAL callback property to decide whether the client is authenticated and authorized to log in. Your callback can retrieve the GSASL_AUTHZID property to inspect the requested authorization name from the client.

5.2 The ANONYMOUS mechanism

The ANONYMOUS mechanism is used to "authenticate" clients to anonymous services; or rather, just indicate that the client wishes to use the service anonymously. The client sends a token, usually her email address, which serve the purpose of some trace information suitable for log files. The token is not permitted to be empty.

In the client, this mechanism is always enabled, and will send the GSASL_ANONYMOUS_TOKEN property as the trace information to the server.

In the server, this mechanism will invoke the GSASL_VALIDATE_ANONYMOUS callback to decide whether the client should be permitted to log in. Your callback can retrieve the GSASL_ANONYMOUS_TOKEN property to, for example, save it in a log file. The token is normally not used to decide whether the client should be permitted to log in or not.

5.3 The PLAIN mechanism

The PLAIN mechanism uses username and password to authenticate users. Two user names are relevant. The first, the authentication identity, indicates the credential holder, i.e., whom the provided password belongs to. The second, the authorization identity, is typically empty, to indicate that the user requests to log on to the server as herself. However, if the authorization identity is not empty, the server should decide whether the authenticated user may log on as the authorization identity. Normally, only "super-user" accounts such as 'admin' or similar should be allowed this.

In the client, this mechanism is always enabled, and require the GSASL_AUTHID and GSASL_PASSWORD properties. If set, GSASL_AUTHZID will also be used.

In the server, the mechanism is always enabled. Two approaches to authenticate and authorize the client are provided.

In the first approach, the server side of the mechanism will request the GSASL_VALIDATE_SIMPLE callback property to decide whether the client should be accepted or not. The callback may inspect the GSASL_AUTHID, GSASL_AUTHZID, and GSASL_PASSWORD properties. These property values will be normalized.

If the first approach fails (because, e.g., your callback returns 'GSASL_NO_CALLBACK' to signal that it does not implement GSASL_VALIDATE_SIMPLE) the mechanism will continue to query the application for a password, via the GSASL_PASSWORD property. Your callback may use the GSASL_AUTHID and GSASL_AUTHZID properties to select the proper password. The password is then normalized and compared to the client credential.

Which approach to use? If your database stores hashed passwords, you have no option, but must use the first approach. If passwords in your user database are stored in prepared (SASLprep) form, the first approach will be faster. If you do not have prepared passwords available, you can use the second approach to make sure the password is prepared properly before comparison.

5.4 The LOGIN mechanism

The LOGIN mechanism is a non-standard mechanism, and is similar to the PLAIN mechanism except that LOGIN lacks the support for authorization identities. Always use PLAIN instead of LOGIN in new applications.

The callback behaviour is the same as for PLAIN, except that GSASL_AUTHZID is neither used nor required, and that the server does not normalize the password using SASLprep.

See Section A.2 [Use of SASLprep in LOGIN], page 74, for a proposed clarification of the interpretation of a hypothetical LOGIN specification.

5.5 The CRAM-MD5 mechanism

The CRAM-MD5 is a widely used, but officially deprecated (apparently in favor of DIGEST-MD5), challenge-response mechanism that transfers hashed passwords instead of clear text passwords. For insecure channels (e.g., when TLS is not used), it is safer than PLAIN. The CRAM-MD5 mechanism does not support authorization identities; making the relationship between CRAM-MD5 and DIGEST-MD5 similar to the relationship between LOGIN and PLAIN.

The disadvantage with hashed passwords is that the server cannot use normal authentication infrastructures such as PAM, because the server must have access to the correct password in order to validate an authentication attempt.

In the client, this mechanism is always enabled, and it requires the `GSASL_AUTHID` and `GSASL_PASSWORD` properties.

In the server, the mechanism will require the `GSASL_PASSWORD` callback property, which may use the `GSASL_AUTHID` property to determine which users' password should be used. The `GSASL_AUTHID` will be in normalized form. The server will then normalize the returned password, and compare the client response with the computed correct response, and accept the user accordingly.

See Section A.1 [Use of SASLprep in CRAM-MD5], page 74, for a clarification on the interpretation of the CRAM-MD5 specification that this implementation rely on.

5.6 The DIGEST-MD5 mechanism

The DIGEST-MD5 mechanism is based on repeated hashing using MD5, which after the MD5 break may be argued to be weaker than HMAC-MD5, but supports more features. For example, authorization identities and data integrity and privacy protection are supported. Like CRAM-MD5, only a hashed password is transferred. Consequently, DIGEST-MD5 needs access to the correct password (although it may be hashed, another improvement compared to CRAM-MD5) to verify the client response. Alas, this makes it impossible to use, e.g., PAM on the server side.

In the client, this mechanism is always enabled, and it requires the `GSASL_AUTHID`, `GSASL_PASSWORD`, `GSASL_SERVICE`, and `GSASL_HOSTNAME` properties. If set, `GSASL_AUTHZID` and `GSASL_REALM` will also be used.

In the server, the mechanism will first request the `GSASL_DIGEST_MD5_HASHED_PASSWORD` callback property to get the user's hashed password. If the callback doesn't supply a hashed password, the `GSASL_PASSWORD` callback property will be requested. Both callbacks may use the `GSASL_AUTHID`, `GSASL_AUTHZID` and `GSASL_REALM` properties to determine which users' password should be used. The server will then compare the client response with a computed correct response, and accept the user accordingly.

The server uses the `GSASL_QOPS` callback to get the set of quality of protection values to use. By default, it advertises support for authentication (`qop-auth`) only. You can use the callback, for example, to make the server advertise support for authentication with integrity layers.

The client uses the `GSASL_QOP` callback to get the quality of protection value to request. The client must choose one of the QOP values offered by the server (which may be inspected through the `GSASL_QOPS` property). If the client does not return a value, `qop-auth` is used by default.

5.7 The SCRAM-SHA-1 mechanism

The SCRAM-SHA-1 mechanism is designed to provide (almost) the same capabilities as CRAM-MD5 and DIGEST-MD5 but use modern cryptographic techniques such as HMAC-SHA-1 hashing and PKCS#5 PBKDF2 key derivation. SCRAM-SHA-1 supports authorization identities. Like CRAM-MD5 and DIGEST-MD5, only a hashed password is transferred.

Consequently, SCRAM-SHA-1 needs access to the correct password to verify the client response. Channel bindings are supported through the SCRAM-SHA-1-PLUS mechanism.

In the client, the non-PLUS mechanism is always enabled, and it requires the `GSASL_AUTHID` property, and either `GSASL_PASSWORD` or `GSASL_SCRAM_SALTED_PASSWORD`. When the `GSASL_CB_TLS_UNIQUE` property is available, the SCRAM-SHA-1-PLUS mechanism is also available and it will negotiate channel bindings when the server also supports it. If set, `GSASL_AUTHZID` will be used by the client. To be able to return the proper `GSASL_SCRAM_SALTED_PASSWORD` value, the client needs to check the `GSASL_SCRAM_ITER` and `GSASL_SCRAM_SALT` values which are available when the `GSASL_SCRAM_SALTED_PASSWORD` property is queried for.

In the server, the mechanism will require the `GSASL_PASSWORD` callback property, which may use the `GSASL_AUTHID` property to determine which users' password should be used. The `GSASL_AUTHID` will be in normalized form. The server will then normalize the returned password, and compare the client response with the computed correct response, and accept the user accordingly. The server may also set the `GSASL_SCRAM_ITER` and `GSASL_SCRAM_SALT` properties to influence the values to be used by clients to derive a key from a password. When the `GSASL_CB_TLS_UNIQUE` property is set, the SCRAM-SHA-1-PLUS mechanism is supported and is used to negotiate channel bindings.

The `GSASL_CB_TLS_UNIQUE` property signal that this side of the authentication supports channel bindings. Setting the property will enable the SCRAM-SHA-1-PLUS mechanism. For clients, this also instructs the SCRAM-SHA-1 mechanism to tell servers that the client believes the server does not support channel bindings if it is used (remember that clients should otherwise have chosen the SCRAM-SHA-1-PLUS mechanism instead of the SCRAM-SHA-1 mechanism). For servers, it means the SCRAM-SHA-1 mechanism will refuse to authenticate against a client that signals that it believes the server does not support channel bindings.

The SCRAM-SHA-1-PLUS mechanism will never complete authentication successfully if channel bindings are not confirmed.

5.8 The NTLM mechanism

The NTLM is a non-standard mechanism. Do not use it in new applications, and do not expect it to be secure. Currently only the client side is supported.

In the client, this mechanism is always enabled, and it requires the `GSASL_AUTHID` and `GSASL_PASSWORD` properties. It will set the 'domain' field in the NTLM request to the value of `GSASL_REALM`. Some servers reportedly need non-empty but arbitrary values in that field.

5.9 The SECURID mechanism

The SECURID mechanism uses authentication and authorization identity together with a passcode from a hardware token to authenticate users.

In the client, this mechanism is always enabled, and it requires the `GSASL_AUTHID` and `GSASL_PASSCODE` properties. If set, `GSASL_AUTHZID` will also be used. If the server requests it, the `GSASL_PIN` property is also required, and its callback may inspect the `GSASL_SUGGESTED_PIN` property to discover a server-provided PIN to use.

In the server, this mechanism will invoke the `GSASL_VALIDATE_SECURID` callback. The callback may inspect the `GSASL_AUTHID`, `GSASL_AUTHZID`, and `GSASL_PASSCODE` properties.

The callback can return GSASL_SECURID_SERVER_NEED_ADDITIONAL_PASSCODE to ask for another additional passcode from the client. The callback can return GSASL_SECURID_SERVER_NEED_NEW_PIN to ask for a new PIN code from the client, in which case it may also set the GSASL_SUGGESTED_PIN property to indicate a recommended new PIN. If the callbacks is invoked again, after having returned GSASL_SECURID_SERVER_NEED_NEW_PIN, it may also inspect the GSASL_PIN property, in addition to the other properties, to find out the client selected PIN code.

5.10 The GSSAPI mechanism

The GSSAPI mechanism allows you to authenticate using Kerberos V5. The mechanism was originally designed to allow for any GSS-API mechanism to be used, but problems with the protocol made it unpractical and it is today restricted for use with Kerberos V5. See the GS2 mechanism (see Section 5.11 [GS2-KRB5], page 30) for a general solution.

In the client, the mechanism is enabled only if the user has acquired credentials (i.e., a ticket granting ticket), and it requires the GSASL_AUTHID, GSASL_SERVICE, and GSASL_HOSTNAME properties.

In the server, the mechanism requires the GSASL_SERVICE and GSASL_HOSTNAME properties, and it will invoke the GSASL_VALIDATE_GSSAPI callback property in order to validate the user. The callback may inspect the GSASL_AUTHZID and GSASL_GSSAPI_DISPLAY_NAME properties to decide whether to authorize the user. Note that authentication is performed by the GSS-API library.

XXX: explain more about quality of service, maximum buffer size, etc.

5.11 The GS2-KRB5 mechanism

GS2 is a protocol bridge between GSS-API and SASL, and allows every GSS-API mechanism that supports mutual authentication and channel bindings to be used as a SASL mechanism. Currently we support the GS2-KRB5 mechanism, for Kerberos V5 authentication, however our GS2 implementation is flexible enough to easily support other GSS-API mechanism if any gains popularity.

In the client, the mechanism is enabled only if the user has acquired credentials (i.e., a ticket granting ticket), and it requires the GSASL_AUTHID, GSASL_SERVICE, and GSASL_HOSTNAME properties.

In the server, the mechanism requires the GSASL_SERVICE and GSASL_HOSTNAME properties, and it will invoke the GSASL_VALIDATE_GSSAPI callback property in order to validate the user. The callback may inspect the GSASL_AUTHZID and GSASL_GSSAPI_DISPLAY_NAME properties to decide whether to authorize the user. Note that authentication is performed by the GSS-API library.

The GS2 framework supports a variant of each mechanism, called the PLUS variant, which can also bind the authentication to a secure channel through channel bindings. Currently this is not supported by GNU SASL.

5.12 The SAML20 mechanism

The SAML20 mechanism makes it possible to use SAML in SASL, in a way that offloads the authentication exchange to an external browser. The protocol implemented is as specified in RFC 6595.

The mechanism makes use of the following properties: `GSASL_AUTHZID`, `GSASL_SAML20_IDP_IDENTIFIER`, `GSASL_SAML20_REDIRECT_URL`, `GSASL_SAML20_AUTHENTICATE_IN_BROWSER` and `GSASL_VALIDATE_SAML20`.

In client mode, the mechanism will retrieve the `GSASL_AUTHZID` and `GSASL_SAML20_IDP_IDENTIFIER` properties and form a request to the server. The server will respond with a redirect URL stored in the `GSASL_SAML20_REDIRECT_URL` property, which the client can retrieve from the `GSASL_SAML20_AUTHENTICATE_IN_BROWSER` callback. The intention is that the client launches a browser to the given URL, and then proceeds with authentication. The server responds whether authentication was successful or not.

In server mode, the mechanism will invoke the `GSASL_SAML20_REDIRECT_URL` callback and the application can inspect the `GSASL_AUTHZID` and `GSASL_SAML20_IDP_IDENTIFIER` properties when forming the redirect URL. The URL is passed to the client which will hopefully complete authentication in the browser. The server callback `GSASL_VALIDATE_SAML20` should check whether the authentication attempt was successful.

Note that SAML itself is not implemented by the GNU SASL library. On the client side, no SAML knowledge is needed, it is only required on the server side. The client only needs to be able to start a browser accessing the redirect URL. The server side is expected to call a SAML library of your choice to generate the AuthRequest and to implement an AssertionConsumerService to validate the AuthResponse. There is a complete proof-of-concept example of a SMTP server with SAML 2.0 support distributed with GNU SASL in the examples/saml20/ sub-directory. It uses the Lasso SAML implementation (`http://lasso.entrouvert.org/`). The example may be used as inspiration for your own server implementation. The **gsasl** command line client supports SAML20 as a client.

5.13 The OPENID20 mechanism

The OPENID20 mechanism makes it possible to use OpenID in SASL, in a way that offloads the authentication exchange to an external browser. The protocol implemented is as specified in RFC 6616.

The mechanism makes use of the following properties: `GSASL_AUTHID` (for the OpenID User-Supplied Identifier), `GSASL_AUTHZID`, `GSASL_OPENID20_REDIRECT_URL`, `GSASL_OPENID20_OUTCOME_DATA`, `GSASL_OPENID20_AUTHENTICATE_IN_BROWSER`, and `GSASL_VALIDATE_OPENID20`.

In the client, the mechanism is enabled by default. The `GSASL_AUTHID` property is required and should contain the User-Supplied OpenID Identifier (for example `http://josefsson.org`). If set, `GSASL_AUTHZID` will be used by the client. The client will be invoked with the `GSASL_OPENID20_AUTHENTICATE_IN_BROWSER` callback to perform the OpenID authentication in a web browser. The callback can retrieve the `GSASL_OPENID20_REDIRECT_URL` property to find out the URL to redirect the user to. After authentication, the client can retrieve the `GSASL_OPENID20_OUTCOME_DATA` property with the OpenID Simple Registry (SREG) attributes sent by the server (they are not always sent).

In the server, the mechanism is enabled by default. The server will request the `GSASL_OPENID20_REDIRECT_URL` property, and your callback may inspect the `GSASL_AUTHID` to find the OpenID User-Supplied Identifier. The server callback should perform OpenID discovery and return the URL to redirect the user to. After this, the user would access the URL and proceed with authentication in the browser. The server is invoked with the `GSASL_VALIDATE_OPENID20` callback to perform the actual validation of the authentication. Usually the callback will perform some IPC communication with an OpenID consumer running in a web server. The callback should return `GSASL_OK` on successful authentication and `GSASL_AUTHENTICATION_ERROR` on authentication errors, or any other error code. If the server received some OpenID Simple Registry (SREG) attributes from the OpenID Identity Provider, it may use the `GSASL_OPENID20_OUTCOME_DATA` property to send these to the client.

Note that OpenID itself is not implemented by the GNU SASL library. On the client side, no OpenID knowledge is required, it is only required on the server side. The client only needs to be able to start a browser accessing the redirect URL. The server side is expected to use an OpenID library of your choice to generate the redirect URL and to implement the Service Provider to validate the response from the IdP. There is a complete proof-of-concept example with a SMTP server with OpenID 2.0 support distributed with GNU SASL in the examples/openid20/ sub-directory. It uses the JanRain PHP5 OpenID implementation. The example may be used as inspiration for your own server implementation. The `gsasl` command line client supports OPENID20 as a client.

5.14 The KERBEROS_V5 mechanism

The KERBEROS_V5 is an experimental mechanism, the protocol specification is available on the GNU SASL homepage. It can operate in three modes, non-infrastructure mode, infrastructure mode and proxied infrastructure mode. Currently only non-infrastructure mode is supported.

In the non-infrastructure mode, it works as a superset of most features provided by PLAIN, CRAM-MD5, DIGEST-MD5 and GSSAPI while at the same time building on what is believed to be proven technology (the RFC 1510 network security system). In the non-infrastructure mode, the client must specify (via callbacks) the name of the user, and optionally the server name and realm. The server must be able to retrieve passwords given the name of the user.

In the infrastructure mode (proxied or otherwise), it allows clients and servers to authenticate via SASL in an RFC 1510 environment, using a trusted third party, a "Key Distribution Central". In the normal mode, clients acquire tickets out of band and then invokes a one roundtrip AP-REQ and AP-REP exchange. In the proxied mode, which can be used by clients without IP addresses or without connectivity to the KDC (e.g., when the KDC is IPv4 and the client is IPV6-only), the client uses the server to proxy ticket requests and finishes with the AP-REQ/AP-REP exchange. In infrastructure mode (proxied or otherwise), neither the client nor server need to implement any callbacks (this will likely change later, to allow a server to authorize users, similar to the GSSAPI callback).

XXX: update when implementation has matured

6 Global Functions

gsasl_init

int gsasl_init (*Gsasl* ** **ctx**)   [Function]
>   *ctx*: pointer to libgsasl handle.
>
>   This functions initializes libgsasl. The handle pointed to by ctx is valid for use with other libgsasl functions iff this function is successful. It also register all builtin SASL mechanisms, using **gsasl_register**().
>
>   **Return value:** GSASL_OK iff successful, otherwise GSASL_MALLOC_ERROR.

gsasl_done

void gsasl_done (*Gsasl* * **ctx**)   [Function]
>   *ctx*: libgsasl handle.
>
>   This function destroys a libgsasl handle. The handle must not be used with other libgsasl functions after this call.

gsasl_client_mechlist

int gsasl_client_mechlist (*Gsasl* * **ctx**, *char* ** **out**)   [Function]
>   *ctx*: libgsasl handle.
>
>   *out*: newly allocated output character array.
>
>   Return a newly allocated string containing SASL names, separated by space, of mechanisms supported by the libgsasl client. **out** is allocated by this function, and it is the responsibility of caller to deallocate it.
>
>   **Return value:** Returns GSASL_OK if successful, or error code.

gsasl_server_mechlist

int gsasl_server_mechlist (*Gsasl* * **ctx**, *char* ** **out**)   [Function]
>   *ctx*: libgsasl handle.
>
>   *out*: newly allocated output character array.
>
>   Return a newly allocated string containing SASL names, separated by space, of mechanisms supported by the libgsasl server. **out** is allocated by this function, and it is the responsibility of caller to deallocate it.
>
>   **Return value:** Returns GSASL_OK if successful, or error code.

gsasl_client_support_p

int gsasl_client_support_p (*Gsasl* * **ctx**, *const char* * **name**)   [Function]
>   *ctx*: libgsasl handle.
>
>   *name*: name of SASL mechanism.
>
>   Decide whether there is client-side support for a specified mechanism.
>
>   **Return value:** Returns 1 if the libgsasl client supports the named mechanism, otherwise 0.

gsasl_server_support_p

int gsasl_server_support_p (*Gsasl* * **ctx**, *const char* * **name**)   [Function]
>   *ctx*: libgsasl handle.
>
>   *name*: name of SASL mechanism.
>
>   Decide whether there is server-side support for a specified mechanism.
>
>   **Return value:** Returns 1 if the libgsasl server supports the named mechanism, otherwise 0.

gsasl_client_suggest_mechanism

const char * gsasl_client_suggest_mechanism (*Gsasl* * **ctx**,   [Function]
>   *const char* * **mechlist**)
>   *ctx*: libgsasl handle.
>
>   *mechlist*: input character array with SASL mechanism names, separated by invalid characters (e.g. SPC).
>
>   Given a list of mechanisms, suggest which to use.
>
>   **Return value:** Returns name of "best" SASL mechanism supported by the libgsasl client which is present in the input string, or NULL if no supported mechanism is found.

gsasl_register

int gsasl_register (*Gsasl* * **ctx**, *const Gsasl_mechanism* * **mech**)   [Function]
>   *ctx*: pointer to libgsasl handle.
>
>   *mech*: plugin structure with information about plugin.
>
>   This function initialize given mechanism, and if successful, add it to the list of plugins that is used by the library.
>
>   **Return value:** GSASL_OK iff successful, otherwise GSASL_MALLOC_ERROR.
>
>   **Since:** 0.2.0

7 Callback Functions

The callback is used by mechanisms to retrieve information, such as username and password, from the application. In a server, the callback is used to decide whether a user is permitted to log in or not. You tell the library of your callback function by calling `gsasl_callback_set`.

Since your callback may need access to data from other parts of your application, there are hooks to store and retrieve application specific pointers. This avoids the use of global variables, which wouldn't be thread safe. You store a pointer to some information (opaque from the point of view of the library) by calling `gsasl_callback_hook_set` and can later retrieve this data in your callback by calling `gsasl_callback_hook_get`.

gsasl_callback_set

void **gsasl_callback_set** (*Gsasl * ctx, Gsasl_callback_function cb*)   [Function]
    ctx: handle received from `gsasl_init()`.

    cb: pointer to function implemented by application.

    Store the pointer to the application provided callback in the library handle. The callback will be used, via `gsasl_callback()`, by mechanisms to discover various parameters (such as username and passwords). The callback function will be called with a Gsasl_property value indicating the requested behaviour. For example, for `GSASL_ANONYMOUS_TOKEN`, the function is expected to invoke gsasl_property_set(CTX, `GSASL_ANONYMOUS_TOKEN`, "token") where "token" is the anonymous token the application wishes the SASL mechanism to use. See the manual for the meaning of all parameters.

    Since: 0.2.0

gsasl_callback

int **gsasl_callback** (*Gsasl * ctx, Gsasl_session * sctx, Gsasl_property*   [Function]
    prop)
    ctx: handle received from `gsasl_init()`, may be NULL to derive it from `sctx`.

    sctx: session handle.

    prop: enumerated value of Gsasl_property type.

    Invoke the application callback. The `prop` value indicate what the callback is expected to do. For example, for `GSASL_ANONYMOUS_TOKEN`, the function is expected to invoke gsasl_property_set(SCTX, `GSASL_ANONYMOUS_TOKEN`, "token") where "token" is the anonymous token the application wishes the SASL mechanism to use. See the manual for the meaning of all parameters.

    Note that if no callback has been set by the application, but the obsolete callback interface has been used, this function will translate the old callback interface into the new. This interface should be sufficient to invoke all callbacks, both new and old.

    Return value: Returns whatever the application callback returns, or `GSASL_NO_CALLBACK` if no application was known.

    Since: 0.2.0

gsasl_callback_hook_set

void **gsasl_callback_hook_set** (*Gsasl * ctx*, *void * hook*)   [Function]
   ctx: libgsasl handle.

   hook: opaque pointer to application specific data.

   Store application specific data in the libgsasl handle.

   The application data can be later (for instance, inside a callback) be retrieved by
   calling **gsasl_callback_hook_get()**. This is normally used by the application to
   maintain a global state between the main program and callbacks.

   Since: 0.2.0

gsasl_callback_hook_get

void * **gsasl_callback_hook_get** (*Gsasl * ctx*)   [Function]
   ctx: libgsasl handle.

   Retrieve application specific data from libgsasl handle.

   The application data is set using **gsasl_callback_hook_set()**. This is normally
   used by the application to maintain a global state between the main program and
   callbacks.

   Return value: Returns the application specific data, or NULL.

   Since: 0.2.0

gsasl_session_hook_set

void **gsasl_session_hook_set** (*Gsasl_session * sctx*, *void * hook*)   [Function]
   sctx: libgsasl session handle.

   hook: opaque pointer to application specific data.

   Store application specific data in the libgsasl session handle.

   The application data can be later (for instance, inside a callback) be retrieved by
   calling **gsasl_session_hook_get()**. This is normally used by the application to
   maintain a per-session state between the main program and callbacks.

   Since: 0.2.14

gsasl_session_hook_get

void * **gsasl_session_hook_get** (*Gsasl_session * sctx*)   [Function]
   sctx: libgsasl session handle.

   Retrieve application specific data from libgsasl session handle.

   The application data is set using **gsasl_callback_hook_set()**. This is normally
   used by the application to maintain a per-session state between the main program
   and callbacks.

   Return value: Returns the application specific data, or NULL.

   Since: 0.2.14

8 Property Functions

gsasl_property_set

void **gsasl_property_set** (*Gsasl_session* * **sctx**, *Gsasl_property* **prop**,   [Function]
         const char * **data**)

sctx: session handle.

   prop: enumerated value of Gsasl_property type, indicating the type of data in **data**.

   data: zero terminated character string to store.

   Make a copy of **data** and store it in the session handle for the indicated property **prop**.

   You can immediately deallocate **data** after calling this function, without affecting the data stored in the session handle.

   Since: 0.2.0

gsasl_property_set_raw

void **gsasl_property_set_raw** (*Gsasl_session* * **sctx**, *Gsasl_property*   [Function]
         prop, *const char* * **data**, *size_t* **len**)

sctx: session handle.

   prop: enumerated value of Gsasl_property type, indicating the type of data in **data**.

   data: character string to store.

   len: length of character string to store.

   Make a copy of **len** sized **data** and store a zero terminated version of it in the session handle for the indicated property **prop**.

   You can immediately deallocate **data** after calling this function, without affecting the data stored in the session handle.

   Except for the length indicator, this function is identical to gsasl_property_set.

   Since: 0.2.0

gsasl_property_fast

const char * **gsasl_property_fast** (*Gsasl_session* * **sctx**,   [Function]
         Gsasl_property **prop**)

sctx: session handle.

   prop: enumerated value of Gsasl_property type, indicating the type of data in **data**.

   Retrieve the data stored in the session handle for given property **prop**.

   The pointer is to live data, and must not be deallocated or modified in any way.

   This function will not invoke the application callback.

   Return value: Return property value, if known, or NULL if no value known.

   Since: 0.2.0

gsasl_property_get

const char * gsasl_property_get (*Gsasl_session* * **sctx**,   [Function]
        Gsasl_property **prop**)

sctx: session handle.

prop: enumerated value of Gsasl_property type, indicating the type of data in `data`.

Retrieve the data stored in the session handle for given property `prop`, possibly invoking the application callback to get the value.

The pointer is to live data, and must not be deallocated or modified in any way.

This function will invoke the application callback, using `gsasl_callback()`, when a property value is not known.

If no value is known, and no callback is specified or if the callback fail to return data, and if any obsolete callback functions has been set by the application, this function will try to call these obsolete callbacks, and store the returned data as the corresponding property. This behaviour of this function will be removed when the obsolete callback interfaces are removed.

Return value: Return data for property, or NULL if no value known.

Since: 0.2.0

9 Session Functions

gsasl_client_start

int gsasl_client_start (*Gsasl* * ctx, *const char* * mech,   [Function]
    Gsasl_session ** sctx)

    ctx: libgsasl handle.

    mech: name of SASL mechanism.

    sctx: pointer to client handle.

    This functions initiates a client SASL authentication. This function must be called
    before any other gsasl_client_*() function is called.

    Return value: Returns GSASL_OK if successful, or error code.

gsasl_server_start

int gsasl_server_start (*Gsasl* * ctx, *const char* * mech,   [Function]
    Gsasl_session ** sctx)

    ctx: libgsasl handle.

    mech: name of SASL mechanism.

    sctx: pointer to server handle.

    This functions initiates a server SASL authentication. This function must be called
    before any other gsasl_server_*() function is called.

    Return value: Returns GSASL_OK if successful, or error code.

gsasl_step

int gsasl_step (*Gsasl_session* * sctx, *const char* * input, *size_t*   [Function]
    input_len, *char* ** output, *size_t* * output_len)

    sctx: libgsasl session handle.

    input: input byte array.

    input_len: size of input byte array.

    output: newly allocated output byte array.

    output_len: pointer to output variable with size of output byte array.

    Perform one step of SASL authentication. This reads data from the other end (from
    input and input_len), processes it (potentially invoking callbacks to the application),
    and writes data to server (into newly allocated variable output and output_len that
    indicate the length of output).

    The contents of the output buffer is unspecified if this functions returns anything
    other than GSASL_OK or GSASL_NEEDS_MORE. If this function return GSASL_OK or
    GSASL_NEEDS_MORE, however, the output buffer is allocated by this function, and it
    is the responsibility of caller to deallocate it by calling free (output).

    Return value: Returns GSASL_OK if authenticated terminated successfully, GSASL_
    NEEDS_MORE if more data is needed, or error code.

gsasl_step64

int **gsasl_step64** (*Gsasl_session* * **sctx**, *const char* * **b64input**, *char*   [Function]
        ** **b64output**)

sctx: libgsasl client handle.

b64input: input base64 encoded byte array.

b64output: newly allocated output base64 encoded byte array.

This is a simple wrapper around **gsasl_step()** that base64 decodes the input and base64 encodes the output.

The contents of the **b64output** buffer is unspecified if this functions returns anything other than **GSASL_OK** or **GSASL_NEEDS_MORE**. If this function return **GSASL_OK** or **GSASL_NEEDS_MORE**, however, the **b64output** buffer is allocated by this function, and it is the responsibility of caller to deallocate it by calling free (**b64output**).

Return value: Returns **GSASL_OK** if authenticated terminated successfully, **GSASL_NEEDS_MORE** if more data is needed, or error code.

gsasl_finish

void **gsasl_finish** (*Gsasl_session* * **sctx**)   [Function]
        sctx: libgsasl session handle.

Destroy a libgsasl client or server handle. The handle must not be used with other libgsasl functions after this call.

gsasl_encode

int **gsasl_encode** (*Gsasl_session* * **sctx**, *const char* * **input**, *size_t*   [Function]
        input_len, *char* ** **output**, *size_t* * **output_len**)
        sctx: libgsasl session handle.

input: input byte array.

input_len: size of input byte array.

output: newly allocated output byte array.

output_len: size of output byte array.

Encode data according to negotiated SASL mechanism. This might mean that data is integrity or privacy protected.

The **output** buffer is allocated by this function, and it is the responsibility of caller to deallocate it by calling free(**output**).

Return value: Returns **GSASL_OK** if encoding was successful, otherwise an error code.

gsasl_decode

int **gsasl_decode** (*Gsasl_session* * **sctx**, *const char* * **input**, *size_t*   [Function]
        input_len, *char* ** **output**, *size_t* * **output_len**)
        sctx: libgsasl session handle.

input: input byte array.

input_len: size of input byte array.

output: newly allocated output byte array.

output_len: size of output byte array.

Decode data according to negotiated SASL mechanism. This might mean that data is integrity or privacy protected.

The `output` buffer is allocated by this function, and it is the responsibility of caller to deallocate it by calling free(`output`).

Return value: Returns `GSASL_OK` if encoding was successful, otherwise an error code.

gsasl_mechanism_name

`const char * gsasl_mechanism_name` (*Gsasl_session * sctx*)   [Function]
    sctx: libgsasl session handle.

    This function returns the name of the SASL mechanism used in the session.

    Return value: Returns a zero terminated character array with the name of the SASL mechanism, or NULL if not known.

    Since: 0.2.28

10 Utilities

gsasl_saslprep

int gsasl_saslprep (*const char * in*, *Gsasl_saslprep_flags* **flags**, *char*   [Function]
    ** out, *int * **stringpreprc**)

in: a UTF-8 encoded string.

flags: any SASLprep flag, e.g., GSASL_ALLOW_UNASSIGNED.

out: on exit, contains newly allocated output string.

stringpreprc: if non-NULL, will hold precise stringprep return code.

Prepare string using SASLprep. On success, the out variable must be deallocated by
the caller.

Return value: Returns GSASL_OK on success, or GSASL_SASLPREP_ERROR on error.

Since: 0.2.3

gsasl_base64_to

int gsasl_base64_to (*const char * in*, *size_t* **inlen**, *char ** out*, *size_t*   [Function]
    * **outlen**)

in: input byte array

inlen: size of input byte array

out: pointer to newly allocated output byte array

outlen: pointer to size of newly allocated output byte array

Encode data as base64. The string is zero terminated, and outlen holds the length
excluding the terminating zero. The out buffer must be deallocated by the caller.

Return value: Returns GSASL_OK on success, or GSASL_MALLOC_ERROR if input was
too large or memory allocation fail.

Since: 0.2.2

gsasl_base64_from

int gsasl_base64_from (*const char * in*, *size_t* **inlen**, *char ** out*,   [Function]
    *size_t * **outlen**)

in: input byte array

inlen: size of input byte array

out: pointer to newly allocated output byte array

outlen: pointer to size of newly allocated output byte array

Decode Base64 data. The out buffer must be deallocated by the caller.

Return value: Returns GSASL_OK on success, GSASL_BASE64_ERROR if input was invalid, and GSASL_MALLOC_ERROR on memory allocation errors.

Since: 0.2.2

gsasl_simple_getpass

int **gsasl_simple_getpass** (*const char* * `filename`, *const char* *   [Function]
    `username`, *char* ** `key`)

filename: filename of file containing passwords.

username: username string.

key: newly allocated output character array.

Retrieve password for user from specified file. The buffer `key` contain the password
if this function is successful. The caller is responsible for deallocating it.

The file should be on the UoW "MD5 Based Authentication" format, which means
it is in text format with comments denoted by # first on the line, with user entries
looking as "usernameTABpassword". This function removes CR and LF at the end
of lines before processing. TAB, CR, and LF denote ASCII values 9, 13, and 10,
respectively.

Return value: Return `GSASL_OK` if output buffer contains the password, `GSASL_AUTHENTICATION_ERROR` if the user could not be found, or other error code.

gsasl_nonce

int **gsasl_nonce** (*char* * `data`, *size_t* `datalen`)   [Function]
    data: output array to be filled with unpredictable random data.

datalen: size of output array.

Store unpredictable data of given size in the provided buffer.

Return value: Returns `GSASL_OK` iff successful.

gsasl_random

int **gsasl_random** (*char* * `data`, *size_t* `datalen`)   [Function]
    data: output array to be filled with strong random data.

datalen: size of output array.

Store cryptographically strong random data of given size in the provided buffer.

Return value: Returns `GSASL_OK` iff successful.

gsasl_md5

int **gsasl_md5** (*const char* * `in`, *size_t* `inlen`, *char* * `out[16]`)   [Function]
    in: input character array of data to hash.

inlen: length of input character array of data to hash.

Compute hash of data using MD5. The `out` buffer must be deallocated by the caller.

Return value: Returns `GSASL_OK` iff successful.

gsasl_hmac_md5

int gsasl_hmac_md5 (*const char* * key, *size_t* keylen, *const char* * in,   [Function]
        size_t inlen, *char* * outhash[16])
> *key*: input character array with key to use.
>
> *keylen*: length of input character array with key to use.
>
> *in*: input character array of data to hash.
>
> *inlen*: length of input character array of data to hash.
>
> Compute keyed checksum of data using HMAC-MD5. The outhash buffer must be deallocated by the caller.
>
> **Return value:** Returns GSASL_OK iff successful.

gsasl_sha1

int gsasl_sha1 (*const char* * in, *size_t* inlen, *char* * out[20])   [Function]
> *in*: input character array of data to hash.
>
> *inlen*: length of input character array of data to hash.
>
> Compute hash of data using SHA1. The out buffer must be deallocated by the caller.
>
> **Return value:** Returns GSASL_OK iff successful.
>
> **Since:** 1.3

gsasl_hmac_sha1

int gsasl_hmac_sha1 (*const char* * key, *size_t* keylen, *const char* * in,   [Function]
        size_t inlen, *char* * outhash[20])
> *key*: input character array with key to use.
>
> *keylen*: length of input character array with key to use.
>
> *in*: input character array of data to hash.
>
> *inlen*: length of input character array of data to hash.
>
> Compute keyed checksum of data using HMAC-SHA1. The outhash buffer must be deallocated by the caller.
>
> **Return value:** Returns GSASL_OK iff successful.
>
> **Since:** 1.3

11 Memory Handling

gsasl_free

void **gsasl_free** (*void * ptr*)   [Function]

>   *ptr*: memory pointer

>   Invoke free(ptr) to de-allocate memory pointer. Typically used on strings allocated by other libgsasl functions.

>   This is useful on Windows where libgsasl is linked to one CRT and the application is linked to another CRT. Then malloc/free will not use the same heap. This happens if you build libgsasl using mingw32 and the application with Visual Studio.

>   **Since:** 0.2.19

12 Error Handling

Most functions in the GNU SASL Library return an error if they fail. For this reason, the application should always catch the error condition and take appropriate measures, for example by releasing the resources and passing the error up to the caller, or by displaying a descriptive message to the user and cancelling the operation.

Some error values do not indicate a system error or an error in the operation, but the result of an operation that failed properly.

12.1 Error values

Errors are returned as `int` values.

The value of the symbol `GSASL_OK` is guaranteed to always be 0, and all other error codes are guaranteed to be non-0, so you may use that information to build boolean expressions involving return codes. Otherwise, an application should not depend on the particular value for error codes, and are encouraged to use the constants even for `GSASL_OK` to improve readability. Possible values are:

`GSASL_OK`   Libgsasl success

`GSASL_NEEDS_MORE`
          SASL mechanism needs more data

`GSASL_UNKNOWN_MECHANISM`
          Unknown SASL mechanism

`GSASL_MECHANISM_CALLED_TOO_MANY_TIMES`
          SASL mechanism called too many times

`GSASL_TOO_SMALL_BUFFER`
          SASL function needs larger buffer (internal error)

`GSASL_FOPEN_ERROR`
          Could not open file in SASL library

`GSASL_FCLOSE_ERROR`
          Could not close file in SASL library

`GSASL_MALLOC_ERROR`
          Memory allocation error in SASL library

`GSASL_BASE64_ERROR`
          Base 64 coding error in SASL library

`GSASL_CRYPTO_ERROR`
          Low-level crypto error in SASL library

`GSASL_NEED_CLIENT_ANONYMOUS_CALLBACK`
          SASL mechanism needs gsasl_client_callback_anonymous() callback (application error)

`GSASL_NEED_CLIENT_PASSWORD_CALLBACK`
          SASL mechanism needs gsasl_client_callback_password() callback (application error)

`GSASL_NEED_CLIENT_PASSCODE_CALLBACK`

> SASL mechanism needs gsasl_client_callback_passcode() callback (application error)

`GSASL_NEED_CLIENT_PIN_CALLBACK`

> SASL mechanism needs gsasl_client_callback_pin() callback (application error)

`GSASL_NEED_CLIENT_AUTHORIZATION_ID_CALLBACK`

> SASL mechanism needs gsasl_client_callback_authorization_id() callback (application error)

`GSASL_NEED_CLIENT_AUTHENTICATION_ID_CALLBACK`

> SASL mechanism needs gsasl_client_callback_authentication_id() callback (application error)

`GSASL_NEED_CLIENT_SERVICE_CALLBACK`

> SASL mechanism needs gsasl_client_callback_service() callback (application error)

`GSASL_NEED_SERVER_VALIDATE_CALLBACK`

> SASL mechanism needs gsasl_server_callback_validate() callback (application error)

`GSASL_NEED_SERVER_CRAM_MD5_CALLBACK`

> SASL mechanism needs gsasl_server_callback_cram_md5() callback (application error)

`GSASL_NEED_SERVER_DIGEST_MD5_CALLBACK`

> SASL mechanism needs gsasl_server_callback_digest_md5() callback (application error)

`GSASL_NEED_SERVER_EXTERNAL_CALLBACK`

> SASL mechanism needs gsasl_server_callback_external() callback (application error)

`GSASL_NEED_SERVER_ANONYMOUS_CALLBACK`

> SASL mechanism needs gsasl_server_callback_anonymous() callback (application error)

`GSASL_NEED_SERVER_REALM_CALLBACK`

> SASL mechanism needs gsasl_server_callback_realm() callback (application error)

`GSASL_NEED_SERVER_SECURID_CALLBACK`

> SASL mechanism needs gsasl_server_callback_securid() callback (application error)

`GSASL_NEED_SERVER_SERVICE_CALLBACK`

> SASL mechanism needs gsasl_server_callback_service() callback (application error)

`GSASL_NEED_SERVER_GSSAPI_CALLBACK`

> SASL mechanism needs gsasl_server_callback_gssapi() callback (application error)

GSASL_NEED_SERVER_RETRIEVE_CALLBACK
>   SASL mechanism needs gsasl_server_callback_retrieve() callback (application error)

GSASL_UNICODE_NORMALIZATION_ERROR
>   Failed to perform Unicode Normalization on string.

GSASL_SASLPREP_ERROR
>   Could not prepare internationalized (non-ASCII) string.

GSASL_MECHANISM_PARSE_ERROR
>   SASL mechanism could not parse input

GSASL_AUTHENTICATION_ERROR
>   Error authenticating user

GSASL_CANNOT_GET_CTX
>   Cannot get internal library handle (library error)

GSASL_INTEGRITY_ERROR
>   Integrity error in application payload

GSASL_NO_MORE_REALMS
>   No more realms available (non-fatal)

GSASL_NO_CLIENT_CODE
>   Client-side functionality not available in library (application error)

GSASL_NO_SERVER_CODE
>   Server-side functionality not available in library (application error)

GSASL_GSSAPI_RELEASE_BUFFER_ERROR
>   GSSAPI library could not deallocate memory in gss_release_buffer() in SASL library. This is a serious internal error.

GSASL_GSSAPI_IMPORT_NAME_ERROR
>   GSSAPI library could not understand a peer name in gss_import_name() in SASL library. This is most likely due to incorrect service and/or hostnames.

GSASL_GSSAPI_INIT_SEC_CONTEXT_ERROR
>   GSSAPI error in client while negotiating security context in gss_init_sec_context() in SASL library. This is most likely due insufficient credentials or malicious interactions.

GSASL_GSSAPI_ACCEPT_SEC_CONTEXT_ERROR
>   GSSAPI error in server while negotiating security context in gss_accept_sec_context() in SASL library. This is most likely due insufficient credentials or malicious interactions.

GSASL_GSSAPI_UNWRAP_ERROR
>   GSSAPI error while decrypting or decoding data in gss_unwrap() in SASL library. This is most likely due to data corruption.

GSASL_GSSAPI_WRAP_ERROR
>   GSSAPI error while encrypting or encoding data in gss_wrap() in SASL library.

GSASL_GSSAPI_ACQUIRE_CRED_ERROR

GSSAPI error acquiring credentials in gss_acquire_cred() in SASL library. This is most likely due to not having the proper Kerberos key available in /etc/krb5.keytab on the server.

GSASL_GSSAPI_DISPLAY_NAME_ERROR

GSSAPI error creating a display name denoting the client in gss_display_name() in SASL library. This is probably because the client supplied bad data.

GSASL_GSSAPI_UNSUPPORTED_PROTECTION_ERROR

Other entity requested integrity or confidentiality protection in GSSAPI mechanism but this is currently not implemented.

GSASL_KERBEROS_V5_INIT_ERROR

Kerberos V5 initialization failure.

GSASL_KERBEROS_V5_INTERNAL_ERROR

Kerberos V5 internal error.

GSASL_SECURID_SERVER_NEED_ADDITIONAL_PASSCODE

SecurID needs additional passcode.

GSASL_SECURID_SERVER_NEED_NEW_PIN

SecurID needs new pin.

GSASL_INVALID_HANDLE

The provided library handle was invalid (application error)

GSASL_NO_CALLBACK

No callback specified by caller (application error).

GSASL_NO_ANONYMOUS_TOKEN

Authentication failed because the anonymous token was not provided.

GSASL_NO_AUTHID

Authentication failed because the authentication identity was not provided.

GSASL_NO_AUTHZID

Authentication failed because the authorization identity was not provided.

GSASL_NO_PASSWORD

Authentication failed because the password was not provided.

GSASL_NO_PASSCODE

Authentication failed because the passcode was not provided.

GSASL_NO_PIN

Authentication failed because the pin code was not provided.

GSASL_NO_SERVICE

Authentication failed because the service name was not provided.

GSASL_NO_HOSTNAME

Authentication failed because the host name was not provided.

GSASL_GSSAPI_ENCAPSULATE_TOKEN_ERROR

GSSAPI error encapsulating token.

GSASL_GSSAPI_DECAPSULATE_TOKEN_ERROR
>   GSSAPI error decapsulating token.

GSASL_GSSAPI_INQUIRE_MECH_FOR_SASLNAME_ERROR
>   GSSAPI error getting OID for SASL mechanism name.

GSASL_GSSAPI_TEST_OID_SET_MEMBER_ERROR
>   GSSAPI error testing for OID in OID set.

GSASL_GSSAPI_RELEASE_OID_SET_ERROR
>   GSSAPI error releasing OID set.

GSASL_NO_CB_TLS_UNIQUE
>   Authentication failed because a tls-unique CB was not provided.

GSASL_NO_SAML20_IDP_IDENTIFIER
>   Callback failed to provide SAML20 IdP identifier.

GSASL_NO_SAML20_REDIRECT_URL
>   Callback failed to provide SAML20 redirect URL.

GSASL_NO_OPENID20_REDIRECT_URL
>   Callback failed to provide OPENID20 redirect URL.

12.2 Error strings

gsasl_strerror

const char * gsasl_strerror (*int* err)   [Function]
>   *err*: libgsasl error code
>
>   Convert return code to human readable string explanation of the reason for the particular error code.
>
>   This string can be used to output a diagnostic message to the user.
>
>   This function is one of few in the library that can be used without a successful call to gsasl_init().
>
>   **Return value:** Returns a pointer to a statically allocated string containing an explanation of the error code err.

gsasl_strerror_name

const char * gsasl_strerror_name (*int* err)   [Function]
>   *err*: libgsasl error code
>
>   Convert return code to human readable string representing the error code symbol itself. For example, gsasl_strerror_name(GSASL_OK) returns the string "GSASL_OK".
>
>   This string can be used to output a diagnostic message to the user.
>
>   This function is one of few in the library that can be used without a successful call to gsasl_init().
>
>   **Return value:** Returns a pointer to a statically allocated string containing a string version of the error code err, or NULL if the error code is not known.
>
>   **Since:** 0.2.29

13 Examples

This chapter contains example code which illustrates how the GNU SASL Library can be used when writing your own application.

13.1 Example 1

```
/* client.c --- Example SASL client.
 * Copyright (C) 2004-2012 Simon Josefsson
 *
 * This file is part of GNU SASL.
 *
 * This program is free software: you can redistribute it and/or modify
 * it under the terms of the GNU General Public License as published by
 * the Free Software Foundation, either version 3 of the License, or
 * (at your option) any later version.
 *
 * This program is distributed in the hope that it will be useful,
 * but WITHOUT ANY WARRANTY; without even the implied warranty of
 * MERCHANTABILITY or FITNESS FOR A PARTICULAR PURPOSE.  See the
 * GNU General Public License for more details.
 *
 * You should have received a copy of the GNU General Public License
 * along with this program.  If not, see <http://www.gnu.org/licenses/>.
 *
 */

#include <config.h>
#include <stdarg.h>
#include <stdio.h>
#include <stdlib.h>
#include <string.h>

#include <gsasl.h>

static void
client_authenticate (Gsasl_session * session)
{
  char buf[BUFSIZ] = "";
  char *p;
  int rc;

  /* This loop mimics a protocol where the client send data first. */

  do
    {
      /* Generate client output. */
```

```
      rc = gsasl_step64 (session, buf, &p);

      if (rc == GSASL_NEEDS_MORE || rc == GSASL_OK)
        {
          /* If sucessful, print it. */
          printf ("Output:\n%s\n", p);
          gsasl_free (p);
        }

      if (rc == GSASL_NEEDS_MORE)
        {
          /* If the client need more data from server, get it here. */
          printf ("Input base64 encoded data from server:\n");
          p = fgets (buf, sizeof (buf) - 1, stdin);
          if (p == NULL)
            {
              perror ("fgets");
              return;
            }
          if (buf[strlen (buf) - 1] == '\n')
            buf[strlen (buf) - 1] = '\0';
        }
    }
  while (rc == GSASL_NEEDS_MORE);

  printf ("\n");

  if (rc != GSASL_OK)
    {
      printf ("Authentication error (%d): %s\n", rc, gsasl_strerror (rc));
      return;
    }

  /* The client is done.  Here you would typically check if the server
     let the client in.  If not, you could try again. */

  printf ("If server accepted us, we're done.\n");
}

static void
client (Gsasl * ctx)
{
  Gsasl_session *session;
  const char *mech = "PLAIN";
  int rc;

  /* Create new authentication session. */
```

```
  if ((rc = gsasl_client_start (ctx, mech, &session)) != GSASL_OK)
    {
      printf ("Cannot initialize client (%d): %s\n", rc, gsasl_strerror (rc));
      return;
    }

  /* Set username and password in session handle.  This info will be
     lost when this session is deallocated below.  */
  gsasl_property_set (session, GSASL_AUTHID, "jas");
  gsasl_property_set (session, GSASL_PASSWORD, "secret");

  /* Do it. */
  client_authenticate (session);

  /* Cleanup. */
  gsasl_finish (session);
}

int
main (int argc, char *argv[])
{
  Gsasl *ctx = NULL;
  int rc;

  /* Initialize library. */
  if ((rc = gsasl_init (&ctx)) != GSASL_OK)
    {
      printf ("Cannot initialize libgsasl (%d): %s", rc, gsasl_strerror (rc));
      return 1;
    }

  /* Do it. */
  client (ctx);

  /* Cleanup. */
  gsasl_done (ctx);

  return 0;
}
```

13.2 Example 2

```
/* client-serverfirst.c --- Example SASL client, where server send data first.
 * Copyright (C) 2004-2012 Simon Josefsson
 *
 * This file is part of GNU SASL.
 *
```

```
 * This program is free software: you can redistribute it and/or modify
 * it under the terms of the GNU General Public License as published by
 * the Free Software Foundation, either version 3 of the License, or
 * (at your option) any later version.
 *
 * This program is distributed in the hope that it will be useful,
 * but WITHOUT ANY WARRANTY; without even the implied warranty of
 * MERCHANTABILITY or FITNESS FOR A PARTICULAR PURPOSE.  See the
 * GNU General Public License for more details.
 *
 * You should have received a copy of the GNU General Public License
 * along with this program.  If not, see <http://www.gnu.org/licenses/>.
 *
 */

#include <config.h>
#include <stdarg.h>
#include <stdio.h>
#include <stdlib.h>
#include <string.h>

#include <gsasl.h>

static void
client_authenticate (Gsasl_session * session)
{
  char buf[BUFSIZ] = "";
  char *p;
  int rc;

  /* This loop mimics a protocol where the server send data first. */

  do
    {
      printf ("Input base64 encoded data from server:\n");
      p = fgets (buf, sizeof (buf) - 1, stdin);
      if (p == NULL)
        {
          perror ("fgets");
          return;
        }
      if (buf[strlen (buf) - 1] == '\n')
        buf[strlen (buf) - 1] = '\0';

      rc = gsasl_step64 (session, buf, &p);

      if (rc == GSASL_NEEDS_MORE || rc == GSASL_OK)
```

```
          {
            printf ("Output:\n%s\n", p);
            gsasl_free (p);
          }
      }
    while (rc == GSASL_NEEDS_MORE);

    printf ("\n");

    if (rc != GSASL_OK)
      {
        printf ("Authentication error (%d): %s\n", rc, gsasl_strerror (rc));
        return;
      }

    /* The client is done.  Here you would typically check if the server
       let the client in.  If not, you could try again. */

    printf ("If server accepted us, we're done.\n");
}

static void
client (Gsasl * ctx)
{
  Gsasl_session *session;
  const char *mech = "CRAM-MD5";
  int rc;

  /* Create new authentication session. */
  if ((rc = gsasl_client_start (ctx, mech, &session)) != GSASL_OK)
    {
      printf ("Cannot initialize client (%d): %s\n", rc, gsasl_strerror (rc));
      return;
    }

  /* Set username and password in session handle.  This info will be
     lost when this session is deallocated below.  */
  gsasl_property_set (session, GSASL_AUTHID, "jas");
  gsasl_property_set (session, GSASL_PASSWORD, "secret");

  /* Do it. */
  client_authenticate (session);

  /* Cleanup. */
  gsasl_finish (session);
}
```

```
int
main (int argc, char *argv[])
{
  Gsasl *ctx = NULL;
  int rc;

  /* Initialize library. */
  if ((rc = gsasl_init (&ctx)) != GSASL_OK)
    {
      printf ("Cannot initialize libgsasl (%d): %s", rc, gsasl_strerror (rc));
      return 1;
    }

  /* Do it. */
  client (ctx);

  /* Cleanup. */
  gsasl_done (ctx);

  return 0;
}
```

13.3 Example 3

```
/* client-mech.c --- Example SASL client, with a choice of mechanism to use.
 * Copyright (C) 2004-2012 Simon Josefsson
 *
 * This file is part of GNU SASL.
 *
 * This program is free software: you can redistribute it and/or modify
 * it under the terms of the GNU General Public License as published by
 * the Free Software Foundation, either version 3 of the License, or
 * (at your option) any later version.
 *
 * This program is distributed in the hope that it will be useful,
 * but WITHOUT ANY WARRANTY; without even the implied warranty of
 * MERCHANTABILITY or FITNESS FOR A PARTICULAR PURPOSE.  See the
 * GNU General Public License for more details.
 *
 * You should have received a copy of the GNU General Public License
 * along with this program.  If not, see <http://www.gnu.org/licenses/>.
 *
 */

#include <config.h>
#include <stdarg.h>
#include <stdio.h>
```

```c
#include <stdlib.h>
#include <string.h>

#include <gsasl.h>

static void
client_authenticate (Gsasl_session * session)
{
  char buf[BUFSIZ] = "";
  char *p;
  int rc;

  /* This loop mimics a protocol where the server send data first. */

  do
    {
      printf ("Input base64 encoded data from server:\n");
      p = fgets (buf, sizeof (buf) - 1, stdin);
      if (p == NULL)
        {
          perror ("fgets");
          return;
        }
      if (buf[strlen (buf) - 1] == '\n')
        buf[strlen (buf) - 1] = '\0';

      rc = gsasl_step64 (session, buf, &p);

      if (rc == GSASL_NEEDS_MORE || rc == GSASL_OK)
        {
          printf ("Output:\n%s\n", p);
          gsasl_free (p);
        }
    }
  while (rc == GSASL_NEEDS_MORE);

  printf ("\n");

  if (rc != GSASL_OK)
    {
      printf ("Authentication error (%d): %s\n", rc, gsasl_strerror (rc));
      return;
    }

  /* The client is done.  Here you would typically check if the server
     let the client in.  If not, you could try again. */
```

```
      printf ("If server accepted us, we're done.\n");
}

static const char *
client_mechanism (Gsasl * ctx)
{
  static char mech[GSASL_MAX_MECHANISM_SIZE + 1] = "";
  char mechlist[BUFSIZ] = "";
  const char *suggestion;
  char *p;

  printf ("Enter list of server supported mechanisms, separate by SPC:\n");
  p = fgets (mechlist, sizeof (mechlist) - 1, stdin);
  if (p == NULL)
    {
      perror ("fgets");
      return NULL;
    }

  suggestion = gsasl_client_suggest_mechanism (ctx, mechlist);
  if (suggestion)
    printf ("Library suggests use of '%s'.\n", suggestion);

  printf ("Enter mechanism to use:\n");
  p = fgets (mech, sizeof (mech) - 1, stdin);
  if (p == NULL)
    {
      perror ("fgets");
      return NULL;
    }

  mech[strlen (mech) - 1] = '\0';

  return mech;
}

static void
client (Gsasl * ctx)
{
  Gsasl_session *session;
  const char *mech;
  int rc;

  /* Find out which mechanism to use. */
  mech = client_mechanism (ctx);

  /* Create new authentication session. */
```

```
  if ((rc = gsasl_client_start (ctx, mech, &session)) != GSASL_OK)
    {
      printf ("Cannot initialize client (%d): %s\n", rc, gsasl_strerror (rc));
      return;
    }

  /* Set username and password in session handle.  This info will be
     lost when this session is deallocated below.  */
  gsasl_property_set (session, GSASL_AUTHID, "jas");
  gsasl_property_set (session, GSASL_PASSWORD, "secret");

  /* Do it. */
  client_authenticate (session);

  /* Cleanup. */
  gsasl_finish (session);
}

int
main (int argc, char *argv[])
{
  Gsasl *ctx = NULL;
  int rc;

  /* Initialize library. */
  if ((rc = gsasl_init (&ctx)) != GSASL_OK)
    {
      printf ("Cannot initialize libgsasl (%d): %s", rc, gsasl_strerror (rc));
      return 1;
    }

  /* Do it. */
  client (ctx);

  /* Cleanup. */
  gsasl_done (ctx);

  return 0;
}
```

13.4 Example 4

```
/* client-callback.c --- Example SASL client, with callback for user info.
 * Copyright (C) 2004-2012 Simon Josefsson
 *
 * This file is part of GNU SASL.
 *
```

```
 * This program is free software: you can redistribute it and/or modify
 * it under the terms of the GNU General Public License as published by
 * the Free Software Foundation, either version 3 of the License, or
 * (at your option) any later version.
 *
 * This program is distributed in the hope that it will be useful,
 * but WITHOUT ANY WARRANTY; without even the implied warranty of
 * MERCHANTABILITY or FITNESS FOR A PARTICULAR PURPOSE.  See the
 * GNU General Public License for more details.
 *
 * You should have received a copy of the GNU General Public License
 * along with this program.  If not, see <http://www.gnu.org/licenses/>.
 *
 */

#include <config.h>
#include <stdarg.h>
#include <stdio.h>
#include <stdlib.h>
#include <string.h>

#include <gsasl.h>

static void
client_authenticate (Gsasl_session * session)
{
  char buf[BUFSIZ] = "";
  char *p;
  int rc;

  /* This loop mimics a protocol where the server send data first. */

  do
    {
      printf ("Input base64 encoded data from server:\n");
      p = fgets (buf, sizeof (buf) - 1, stdin);
      if (p == NULL)
        {
          perror ("fgets");
          return;
        }
      if (buf[strlen (buf) - 1] == '\n')
        buf[strlen (buf) - 1] = '\0';

      rc = gsasl_step64 (session, buf, &p);

      if (rc == GSASL_NEEDS_MORE || rc == GSASL_OK)
```

```
          {
            printf ("Output:\n%s\n", p);
            gsasl_free (p);
          }
      }
  while (rc == GSASL_NEEDS_MORE);

  printf ("\n");

  if (rc != GSASL_OK)
    {
      printf ("Authentication error (%d): %s\n", rc, gsasl_strerror (rc));
      return;
    }

  /* The client is done.  Here you would typically check if the server
     let the client in.  If not, you could try again. */

  printf ("If server accepted us, we're done.\n");
}

static void
client (Gsasl * ctx)
{
  Gsasl_session *session;
  const char *mech = "SECURID";
  int rc;

  /* Create new authentication session. */
  if ((rc = gsasl_client_start (ctx, mech, &session)) != GSASL_OK)
    {
      printf ("Cannot initialize client (%d): %s\n", rc, gsasl_strerror (rc));
      return;
    }

  /* Do it. */
  client_authenticate (session);

  /* Cleanup. */
  gsasl_finish (session);
}

static int
callback (Gsasl * ctx, Gsasl_session * sctx, Gsasl_property prop)
{
  char buf[BUFSIZ] = "";
  int rc = GSASL_NO_CALLBACK;
```

```
  char *p;

  /* Get user info from user. */

  printf ("Callback invoked, for property %d.\n", prop);

  switch (prop)
    {
    case GSASL_PASSCODE:
      printf ("Enter passcode:\n");
      p = fgets (buf, sizeof (buf) - 1, stdin);
      if (p == NULL)
        {
          perror ("fgets");
          break;
        }
      buf[strlen (buf) - 1] = '\0';

      gsasl_property_set (sctx, GSASL_PASSCODE, buf);
      rc = GSASL_OK;
      break;

    case GSASL_AUTHID:
      printf ("Enter username:\n");
      p = fgets (buf, sizeof (buf) - 1, stdin);
      if (p == NULL)
        {
          perror ("fgets");
          break;
        }
      buf[strlen (buf) - 1] = '\0';

      gsasl_property_set (sctx, GSASL_AUTHID, buf);
      rc = GSASL_OK;
      break;

    default:
      printf ("Unknown property!  Don't worry.\n");
      break;
    }

  return rc;
}

int
main (int argc, char *argv[])
{
```

```
    Gsasl *ctx = NULL;
    int rc;

    /* Initialize library. */
    if ((rc = gsasl_init (&ctx)) != GSASL_OK)
      {
        printf ("Cannot initialize libgsasl (%d): %s", rc, gsasl_strerror (rc));
        return 1;
      }

    /* Set the callback handler for the library. */
    gsasl_callback_set (ctx, callback);

    /* Do it. */
    client (ctx);

    /* Cleanup. */
    gsasl_done (ctx);

    return 0;
}
```

13.5 Example 5

```
/* smtp-server.c --- Example SMTP server with SASL authentication
 * Copyright (C) 2012 Simon Josefsson
 *
 * This file is part of GNU SASL.
 *
 * This program is free software: you can redistribute it and/or modify
 * it under the terms of the GNU General Public License as published by
 * the Free Software Foundation, either version 3 of the License, or
 * (at your option) any later version.
 *
 * This program is distributed in the hope that it will be useful,
 * but WITHOUT ANY WARRANTY; without even the implied warranty of
 * MERCHANTABILITY or FITNESS FOR A PARTICULAR PURPOSE.  See the
 * GNU General Public License for more details.
 *
 * You should have received a copy of the GNU General Public License
 * along with this program.  If not, see <http://www.gnu.org/licenses/>.
 *
 */

/* This is a minimal SMTP server with GNU SASL authentication support.
   The only valid password is "sesam".  This server will complete
   authentications using LOGIN, PLAIN, DIGEST-MD5, CRAM-MD5, and
```

```
                  SCRAM-SHA-1.  It accepts an optional command line parameter
                  specifying the service name (i.e., a numerical port number or
                  /etc/services name).  By default it listens on port "2000".  */

#include <config.h>
#include <string.h>
#include <stdlib.h>
#include <stdarg.h>
#include <netdb.h>
#include <signal.h>

#include <gsasl.h>

static int
callback (Gsasl * ctx, Gsasl_session * sctx, Gsasl_property prop)
{
  int rc = GSASL_NO_CALLBACK;

  switch (prop)
    {
    case GSASL_PASSWORD:
      gsasl_property_set (sctx, prop, "sesam");
      rc = GSASL_OK;
      break;

    default:
      /* You may want to log (at debug verbosity level) that an
         unknown property was requested here, possibly after filtering
         known rejected property requests. */
      break;
    }

  return rc;
}

static ssize_t
gettrimline (char **line, size_t * n, FILE * fh)
{
  ssize_t s = getline (line, n, fh);

  if (s >= 2)
    {
      if ((*line)[strlen (*line) - 1] == '\n')
        (*line)[strlen (*line) - 1] = '\0';
      if ((*line)[strlen (*line) - 1] == '\r')
        (*line)[strlen (*line) - 1] = '\0';
```

```
        printf ("C: %s\n", *line);
      }

  return s;
}

#define print(fh, ...)                                                  \
  printf ("S: "), printf (__VA_ARGS__), fprintf (fh, __VA_ARGS__)

static void
server_auth (FILE * fh, Gsasl_session * session)
{
  char *line = NULL;
  size_t n = 0;
  char *p;
  int rc;

  /* The ordering and the type of checks in the following loop has to
     be adapted for each protocol depending on its SASL properties.
     SMTP is a "server-first" SASL protocol.  This implementation do
     not support piggy-backing of the initial client challenge nor
     piggy-backing of the terminating server response.  See RFC 2554
     and RFC 4422 for terminology.  That profile results in the
     following loop structure.  Ask on the help-gsasl list if you are
     uncertain.  */
  do
    {
      rc = gsasl_step64 (session, line, &p);
      if (rc == GSASL_NEEDS_MORE || (rc == GSASL_OK && p && *p))
        {
          print (fh, "334 %s\n", p);
          gsasl_free (p);

          if (gettrimline (&line, &n, fh) < 0)
            {
              print (fh, "221 localhost getline failure\n");
              goto done;
            }
        }
    }
  while (rc == GSASL_NEEDS_MORE);

  if (rc != GSASL_OK)
    {
      print (fh, "535 gsasl_step64 (%d): %s\n", rc, gsasl_strerror (rc));
      goto done;
    }
```

```
  {
    const char *authid = gsasl_property_fast (session, GSASL_AUTHID);
    const char *authzid = gsasl_property_fast (session, GSASL_AUTHZID);
    print (fh, "235 OK [authid: %s authzid: %s]\n",
           authid ? authid : "N/A", authzid ? authzid : "N/A");
  }

done:
  free (line);
}

static void
smtp (FILE * fh, Gsasl * ctx)
{
  char *line = NULL;
  size_t n = 0;
  int rc;

  print (fh, "220 localhost ESMTP GNU SASL smtp-server\n");

  while (gettrimline (&line, &n, fh) >= 0)
    {
      if (strncmp (line, "EHLO ", 5) == 0 || strncmp (line, "ehlo ", 5) == 0)
        {
          char *mechlist;

          rc = gsasl_server_mechlist (ctx, &mechlist);
          if (rc != GSASL_OK)
            {
              print (fh, "221 localhost gsasl_server_mechlist (%d): %s\n",
                     rc, gsasl_strerror (rc));
              goto done;
            }

          print (fh, "250-localhost\n");
          print (fh, "250 AUTH %s\n", mechlist);

          gsasl_free (mechlist);
        }
      else if (strncmp (line, "AUTH ", 5) == 0
               || strncmp (line, "auth ", 5) == 0)
        {
          Gsasl_session *session = NULL;

          if ((rc = gsasl_server_start (ctx, line + 5, &session)) != GSASL_OK)
            {
```

```
                    print (fh, "221 localhost gsasl_server_start (%d): %s\n",
                          rc, gsasl_strerror (rc));
                    goto done;
                  }

                server_auth (fh, session);

                gsasl_finish (session);
              }
          else if (strncmp (line, "QUIT", 4) == 0
                   || strncmp (line, "quit", 4) == 0)
            {
              print (fh, "221 localhost QUIT\n");
              goto done;
            }
          else
            print (fh, "500 unrecognized command\n");
        }

  print (fh, "221 localhost getline failure\n");

done:
  free (line);
}

int
main (int argc, char *argv[])
{
  const char *service = argc > 1 ? argv[1] : "2000";
  volatile int run = 1;
  struct addrinfo hints, *addrs;
  int sockfd;
  int rc;
  int yes = 1;
  Gsasl *ctx;

  setvbuf (stdout, NULL, _IONBF, 0);

  rc = gsasl_init (&ctx);
  if (rc < 0)
    {
      printf ("gsasl_init (%d): %s\n", rc, gsasl_strerror (rc));
      exit (EXIT_FAILURE);
    }

  printf ("%s [gsasl header %s library %s]\n",
          argv[0], GSASL_VERSION, gsasl_check_version (NULL));
```

```
gsasl_callback_set (ctx, callback);

memset (&hints, 0, sizeof (hints));
hints.ai_flags = AI_PASSIVE | AI_ADDRCONFIG;
hints.ai_socktype = SOCK_STREAM;

rc = getaddrinfo (NULL, service, &hints, &addrs);
if (rc < 0)
  {
    printf ("getaddrinfo: %s\n", gai_strerror (rc));
    exit (EXIT_FAILURE);
  }

sockfd = socket (addrs->ai_family, addrs->ai_socktype, addrs->ai_protocol);
if (sockfd < 0)
  {
    perror ("socket");
    exit (EXIT_FAILURE);
  }

if (setsockopt (sockfd, SOL_SOCKET, SO_REUSEADDR, &yes, sizeof (yes)) < 0)
  {
    perror ("setsockopt");
    exit (EXIT_FAILURE);
  }

rc = bind (sockfd, addrs->ai_addr, addrs->ai_addrlen);
if (rc < 0)
  {
    perror ("bind");
    exit (EXIT_FAILURE);
  }

freeaddrinfo (addrs);

rc = listen (sockfd, SOMAXCONN);
if (rc < 0)
  {
    perror ("listen");
    exit (EXIT_FAILURE);
  }

signal (SIGPIPE, SIG_IGN);

while (run)
  {
```

```
      struct sockaddr from;
      socklen_t fromlen = sizeof (from);
      char host[NI_MAXHOST];
      int fd;
      FILE *fh;

      fd = accept (sockfd, &from, &fromlen);
      if (fd < 0)
        {
          perror ("accept");
          continue;
        }

      rc = getnameinfo (&from, fromlen, host, sizeof (host),
                        NULL, 0, NI_NUMERICHOST);
      if (rc == 0)
        printf ("connection from %s\n", host);
      else
        printf ("getnameinfo: %s\n", gai_strerror (rc));

      fh = fdopen (fd, "w+");
      if (!fh)
        {
          perror ("fdopen");
          close (fd);
          continue;
        }

      smtp (fh, ctx);

      fclose (fh);
    }

  close (sockfd);
  gsasl_done (ctx);

  return 0;
}
```

14 Acknowledgements

The makefiles, manuals, etc borrowed much from Libgcrypt written by Werner Koch.

Cryptographic functions for some SASL mechanisms uses Libgcrypt by Werner Koch et al. The NTLM mechanism uses Libntlm by Grant Edwards et al, using code from Samba written by Andrew Tridgell, and now maintained by Simon Josefsson. The KERBEROS_V5 mechanism uses Shishi by Simon Josefsson. The GSSAPI and GS2-KRB5 mechanism uses a GSS-API implementation, such as GNU GSS by Simon Josefsson.

Gnulib is used to simplify portability.

This manual borrows text from the SASL specification.

15 Invoking gsasl

Name

GNU SASL (gsasl) – Command line interface to libgsasl.

Description

`gsasl` is the main program of GNU SASL.

This section only lists the commands and options available.

Mandatory or optional arguments to long options are also mandatory or optional for any corresponding short options.

Commands

`gsasl` recognizes these commands:

```
-c, --client              Act as client (the default).
    --client-mechanisms   Write name of supported client mechanisms
                          separated by space to stdout.
-s, --server              Act as server.
    --server-mechanisms   Write name of supported server mechanisms
                          separated by space to stdout.
```

Network Options

Normally the SASL negotiation is performed on the terminal, with reading from stdin and writing to stdout. It is also possible to perform the negotiation with a server over a TCP network connection.

```
--connect=HOSTNAME[:SERVICE]
                          Connect to TCP server and negotiate on stream
                          instead of stdin/stdout. SERVICE is the protocol
                          service, or an integer denoting the port, and
                          defaults to 143 (imap) if not specified. Also sets
                          the --hostname default.
```

Miscellaneous Options:

These parameters affect overall behaviour.

```
-d, --application-data    After authentication, read data from stdin and run
                          it through the mechanism's security layer and
                          print it base64 encoded to stdout. The default is
                          to terminate after authentication.
    --imap                Use a IMAP-like logon procedure (client only).
                          Also sets the --service default to "imap".
-m, --mechanism=STRING    Mechanism to use.
    --no-client-first     Disallow client to send data first (client only).
```

SASL Mechanism Options

These options modify the behaviour of the callbacks (see Chapter 7 [Callback Functions], page 35) in the library. The default is to query the user on the terminal.

```
-n, --anonymous-token=STRING    Token for anonymous authentication, usually
                                mail address (ANONYMOUS only).
-a, --authentication-id=STRING  Identity of credential owner.
-z, --authorization-id=STRING   Identity to request service for.
    --disable-cleartext-validate
                                Disable cleartext validate hook, forcing server to
                                prompt for password.
    --enable-cram-md5-validate  Validate CRAM-MD5 challenge and response
                                interactively.
    --hostname=STRING           Set the name of the server with the requested
                                service.
-p, --password=STRING           Password for authentication (insecure for
                                non-testing purposes).
    --passcode=NUMBER           Passcode for authentication (SECURID only).
    --quality-of-protection=<qop-auth | qop-int | qop-conf>
                                How application payload will be protected.
                                "qop-auth" means no protection,
                                "qop-int" means integrity protection,
                                "qop-conf" means confidentiality.
                                Currently only used by DIGEST-MD5, where the
                                default is "qop-int".
-r, --realm=STRING              Realm. Defaults to hostname.
    --service=STRING            Set the requested service name (should be a
                                registered GSSAPI host based service name).
    --service-name=STRING       Set the generic server name in case of a
                                replicated server (DIGEST-MD5 only).
-x, --maxbuf=NUMBER             Indicate maximum buffer size (DIGEST-MD5 only).
```

STARTTLS options

--starttls	Force use of STARTTLS. The default is to use STARTTLS when available. (default=off)
--no-starttls	Unconditionally disable STARTTLS. (default=off)
--no-cb	Don't set any channel bindings. (default=off)
--x509-ca-file=FILE	File containing one or more X.509 Certificate Authorities certificates in PEM format, used to verify the certificate received from the server. If not specified, no verification of the remote server certificate will be done.
--x509-cert-file=FILE	File containing client X.509 certificate in PEM format. Used together with --x509-key-file to specify the certificate/key pair.
--x509-key-file=FILE	Private key for the client X.509 certificate in PEM format. Used together with --x509-key-file to specify the certificate/key pair.
--priority	Cipher priority string.

Other Options

These are some standard parameters.

-q, --quiet, --silent	Don't produce any diagnostic output.
-v, --verbose	Produce verbose output.
-?, --help	Give this help list
--usage	Give a short usage message
-V, --version	Print program version

Appendix A Protocol Clarifications

This appendix contains clarifications to various SASL specification that we felt were necessary to include, if for nothing else it may serve as a guide for other implementers that worry about the same issues.

A.1 Use of SASLprep in CRAM-MD5

The specification, as of 'draft-ietf-sasl-crammd5-04.txt', is silent on whether a SASL server implementation applying SASLprep on a password received from an external, non-SASL specific database (i.e., the passwords are not stored in SASLprep form in the database), should set or clear the AllowUnassigned bit. The motivation for the AU-bit in StringPrep/SASLprep is for stored vs query strings. It could be argued that in this situation the server can treat the external password either as a stored string (from a database) or as a query (the server uses the string as a query into the fixed HMAC-MD5 hash).

The specification is also unclear on whether clients should set or clear the AllowUnassigned flag.

In the server, GNU SASL applies SASLprep to the password with the AllowUnassigned bit cleared.

A.2 Use of SASLprep in LOGIN

The non-standard mechanism LOGIN presumably does not support non-ASCII. We suggest that the client should send unprepared UTF-8 and that the server apply SASLprep with the AllowUnassigned bit cleared on the received username and password.

Appendix B Old Functions

As GNU SASL is still under heavy development, some API functions have been found to be less useful. Those old API functions will be supported during a transition period. Refer to the NEWS file to find out since when a function has been deprecated.

gsasl_client_listmech

int gsasl_client_listmech (*Gsasl* * ctx, *char* * out, *size_t* *   [Function]
    outlen)
> *ctx*: libgsasl handle.
>
> *out*: output character array.
>
> *outlen*: input maximum size of output character array, on output contains actual length of output array.
>
> Write SASL names, separated by space, of mechanisms supported by the libgsasl client to the output array. To find out how large the output array must be, call this function with a NULL out parameter.
>
> **Return value:** Returns GSASL_OK if successful, or error code.
>
> **Deprecated:** Use gsasl_client_mechlist() instead.

gsasl_server_listmech

int gsasl_server_listmech (*Gsasl* * ctx, *char* * out, *size_t* *   [Function]
    outlen)
> *ctx*: libgsasl handle.
>
> *out*: output character array.
>
> *outlen*: input maximum size of output character array, on output contains actual length of output array.
>
> Write SASL names, separated by space, of mechanisms supported by the libgsasl server to the output array. To find out how large the output array must be, call this function with a NULL out parameter.
>
> **Return value:** Returns GSASL_OK if successful, or error code.
>
> **Deprecated:** Use gsasl_server_mechlist() instead.

gsasl_client_step

int gsasl_client_step (*Gsasl_session* * sctx, *const char* * input,   [Function]
    size_t input_len, *char* * output, *size_t* * output_len)
> *sctx*: libgsasl client handle.
>
> *input*: input byte array.
>
> *input_len*: size of input byte array.
>
> *output*: output byte array.
>
> *output_len*: size of output byte array.

Perform one step of SASL authentication in client. This reads data from server (specified with input and input_len), processes it (potentially invoking callbacks to the application), and writes data to server (into variables output and output_len).

The contents of the output buffer is unspecified if this functions returns anything other than GSASL_NEEDS_MORE.

Return value: Returns GSASL_OK if authenticated terminated successfully, GSASL_NEEDS_MORE if more data is needed, or error code.

Deprecated: Use gsasl_step() instead.

gsasl_server_step

int gsasl_server_step (*Gsasl_session* * **sctx**, *const char* * **input**,   [Function]
        size_t **input_len**, *char* * **output**, *size_t* * **output_len**)

sctx: libgsasl server handle.

input: input byte array.

input_len: size of input byte array.

output: output byte array.

output_len: size of output byte array.

Perform one step of SASL authentication in server. This reads data from client (specified with input and input_len), processes it (potentially invoking callbacks to the application), and writes data to client (into variables output and output_len).

The contents of the output buffer is unspecified if this functions returns anything other than GSASL_NEEDS_MORE.

Return value: Returns GSASL_OK if authenticated terminated successfully, GSASL_NEEDS_MORE if more data is needed, or error code.

Deprecated: Use gsasl_step() instead.

gsasl_client_step_base64

int gsasl_client_step_base64 (*Gsasl_session* * **sctx**, *const char* *   [Function]
        b64input, *char* * **b64output**, *size_t* **b64output_len**)

sctx: libgsasl client handle.

b64input: input base64 encoded byte array.

b64output: output base64 encoded byte array.

b64output_len: size of output base64 encoded byte array.

This is a simple wrapper around gsasl_client_step() that base64 decodes the input and base64 encodes the output.

Return value: See gsasl_client_step().

Deprecated: Use gsasl_step64() instead.

gsasl_server_step_base64

int gsasl_server_step_base64 (*Gsasl_session* * sctx, *const char* *   [Function]
    b64input, *char* * b64output, *size_t* b64output_len)

sctx: libgsasl server handle.

b64input: input base64 encoded byte array.

b64output: output base64 encoded byte array.

b64output_len: size of output base64 encoded byte array.

This is a simple wrapper around gsasl_server_step() that base64 decodes the input
and base64 encodes the output.

Return value: See gsasl_server_step().

Deprecated: Use gsasl_step64() instead.

gsasl_client_finish

void gsasl_client_finish (*Gsasl_session* * sctx)   [Function]

sctx: libgsasl client handle.

Destroy a libgsasl client handle. The handle must not be used with other libgsasl
functions after this call.

Deprecated: Use gsasl_finish() instead.

gsasl_server_finish

void gsasl_server_finish (*Gsasl_session* * sctx)   [Function]

sctx: libgsasl server handle.

Destroy a libgsasl server handle. The handle must not be used with other libgsasl
functions after this call.

Deprecated: Use gsasl_finish() instead.

gsasl_client_ctx_get

Gsasl * gsasl_client_ctx_get (*Gsasl_session* * sctx)   [Function]

sctx: libgsasl client handle

Get the libgsasl handle given a libgsasl client handle.

Return value: Returns the libgsasl handle given a libgsasl client handle.

Deprecated: This function is not useful with the new 0.2.0 API.

gsasl_client_application_data_set

void gsasl_client_application_data_set (*Gsasl_session* * sctx,   [Function]
    void * application_data)

sctx: libgsasl client handle.

application_data: opaque pointer to application specific data.

Store application specific data in the libgsasl client handle. The application data
can be later (for instance, inside a callback) be retrieved by calling gsasl_client_
application_data_get(). It is normally used by the application to maintain state
between the main program and the callback.

Deprecated: Use `gsasl_callback_hook_set()` or `gsasl_session_hook_set()` instead.

gsasl_client_application_data_get

void * gsasl_client_application_data_get (*Gsasl_session* *   [Function]
    sctx)

sctx: libgsasl client handle.

Retrieve application specific data from libgsasl client handle. The application data is set using `gsasl_client_application_data_set()`. It is normally used by the application to maintain state between the main program and the callback.

Return value: Returns the application specific data, or NULL.

Deprecated: Use `gsasl_callback_hook_get()` or `gsasl_session_hook_get()` instead.

gsasl_server_ctx_get

Gsasl * gsasl_server_ctx_get (*Gsasl_session* * sctx)   [Function]
    sctx: libgsasl server handle

Get the libgsasl handle given a libgsasl server handle.

Return value: Returns the libgsasl handle given a libgsasl server handle.

Deprecated: This function is not useful with the new 0.2.0 API.

gsasl_server_application_data_set

void gsasl_server_application_data_set (*Gsasl_session* * sctx,   [Function]
    void * application_data)

sctx: libgsasl server handle.

application_data: opaque pointer to application specific data.

Store application specific data in the libgsasl server handle. The application data can be later (for instance, inside a callback) be retrieved by calling `gsasl_server_application_data_get()`. It is normally used by the application to maintain state between the main program and the callback.

Deprecated: Use `gsasl_callback_hook_set()` or `gsasl_session_hook_set()` instead.

gsasl_server_application_data_get

void * gsasl_server_application_data_get (*Gsasl_session* *   [Function]
    sctx)

sctx: libgsasl server handle.

Retrieve application specific data from libgsasl server handle. The application data is set using `gsasl_server_application_data_set()`. It is normally used by the application to maintain state between the main program and the callback.

Return value: Returns the application specific data, or NULL.

Deprecated: Use `gsasl_callback_hook_get()` or `gsasl_session_hook_get()` instead.

gsasl_randomize

int **gsasl_randomize** (*int* `strong`, *char* * `data`, *size_t* `datalen`)   [Function]
> *strong*: 0 iff operation should not block, non-0 for very strong randomness.
>
> *data*: output array to be filled with random data.
>
> *datalen*: size of output array.
>
> Store cryptographically random data of given size in the provided buffer.
>
> **Return value:** Returns `GSASL_OK` iff successful.
>
> **Deprecated:** Use `gsasl_random()` or `gsasl_nonce()` instead.

gsasl_ctx_get

Gsasl * **gsasl_ctx_get** (*Gsasl_session* * `sctx`)   [Function]
> *sctx*: libgsasl session handle
>
> Get the libgsasl handle given a libgsasl session handle.
>
> **Return value:** Returns the libgsasl handle given a libgsasl session handle.
>
> **Deprecated:** This function is not useful with the new 0.2.0 API.

gsasl_encode_inline

int **gsasl_encode_inline** (*Gsasl_session* * `sctx`, *const char* * `input`,   [Function]
        size_t `input_len`, *char* * `output`, *size_t* * `output_len`)
> *sctx*: libgsasl session handle.
>
> *input*: input byte array.
>
> *input_len*: size of input byte array.
>
> *output*: output byte array.
>
> *output_len*: size of output byte array.
>
> Encode data according to negotiated SASL mechanism. This might mean that data is integrity or privacy protected.
>
> **Return value:** Returns `GSASL_OK` if encoding was successful, otherwise an error code.
>
> **Deprecated:** Use `gsasl_encode()` instead.
>
> **Since:** 0.2.0

gsasl_decode_inline

int **gsasl_decode_inline** (*Gsasl_session* * `sctx`, *const char* * `input`,   [Function]
        size_t `input_len`, *char* * `output`, *size_t* * `output_len`)
> *sctx*: libgsasl session handle.
>
> *input*: input byte array.
>
> *input_len*: size of input byte array.
>
> *output*: output byte array.
>
> *output_len*: size of output byte array.
>
> Decode data according to negotiated SASL mechanism. This might mean that data is integrity or privacy protected.

Return value: Returns `GSASL_OK` if encoding was successful, otherwise an error code.

Deprecated: Use `gsasl_decode()` instead.

Since: 0.2.0

gsasl_application_data_set

void gsasl_application_data_set (*Gsasl* * *ctx*, *void* * *appdata*)   [Function]
ctx: libgsasl handle.

appdata: opaque pointer to application specific data.

Store application specific data in the libgsasl handle. The application data can be later (for instance, inside a callback) be retrieved by calling `gsasl_application_data_get()`. It is normally used by the application to maintain state between the main program and the callback.

Deprecated: Use `gsasl_callback_hook_set()` instead.

gsasl_application_data_get

void * gsasl_application_data_get (*Gsasl* * *ctx*)   [Function]
ctx: libgsasl handle.

Retrieve application specific data from libgsasl handle. The application data is set using `gsasl_application_data_set()`. It is normally used by the application to maintain state between the main program and the callback.

Return value: Returns the application specific data, or NULL.

Deprecated: Use `gsasl_callback_hook_get()` instead.

gsasl_appinfo_set

void gsasl_appinfo_set (*Gsasl_session* * *sctx*, *void* * *appdata*)   [Function]
sctx: libgsasl session handle.

appdata: opaque pointer to application specific data.

Store application specific data in the libgsasl session handle. The application data can be later (for instance, inside a callback) be retrieved by calling `gsasl_appinfo_get()`. It is normally used by the application to maintain state between the main program and the callback.

Deprecated: Use `gsasl_callback_hook_set()` instead.

gsasl_appinfo_get

void * gsasl_appinfo_get (*Gsasl_session* * *sctx*)   [Function]
sctx: libgsasl session handle.

Retrieve application specific data from libgsasl session handle. The application data is set using `gsasl_appinfo_set()`. It is normally used by the application to maintain state between the main program and the callback.

Return value: Returns the application specific data, or NULL.

Deprecated: Use `gsasl_callback_hook_get()` instead.

gsasl_server_suggest_mechanism

const char * gsasl_server_suggest_mechanism (*Gsasl* * ctx,   [Function]
    const char * mechlist)

ctx: libgsasl handle.

mechlist: input character array with SASL mechanism names, separated by invalid characters (e.g. SPC).

Get name of "best" SASL mechanism supported by the libgsasl server which is present in the input string.

Return value: Returns name of "best" SASL mechanism supported by the libgsasl server which is present in the input string.

Deprecated: This function was never useful, since it is the client that chose which mechanism to use.

gsasl_client_callback_authentication_id_set

void gsasl_client_callback_authentication_id_set (*Gsasl* *   [Function]
    ctx, *Gsasl_client_callback_authentication_id* cb)

ctx: libgsasl handle.

cb: callback function

Specify the callback function to use in the client to set the authentication identity. The function can be later retrieved using gsasl_client_callback_authentication_id_get().

Deprecated: This function is part of the old callback interface. The new interface uses gsasl_callback_set() to set the application callback, and uses gsasl_callback() or gsasl_property_get() to invoke the callback for certain properties.

gsasl_client_callback_authentication_id_get

Gsasl_client_callback_authentication_id   [Function]
    gsasl_client_callback_authentication_id_get (*Gsasl* * ctx)

ctx: libgsasl handle.

Get the callback earlier set by calling gsasl_client_callback_authentication_id_set().

Return value: Returns the callback earlier set by calling gsasl_client_callback_authentication_id_set().

Deprecated: This function is part of the old callback interface. The new interface uses gsasl_callback_set() to set the application callback, and uses gsasl_callback() or gsasl_property_get() to invoke the callback for certain properties.

gsasl_client_callback_authorization_id_set

void gsasl_client_callback_authorization_id_set (*Gsasl* * ctx,   [Function]
    Gsasl_client_callback_authorization_id cb)

ctx: libgsasl handle.

cb: callback function

Specify the callback function to use in the client to set the authorization identity. The function can be later retrieved using `gsasl_client_callback_authorization_id_get()`.

Deprecated: This function is part of the old callback interface. The new interface uses `gsasl_callback_set()` to set the application callback, and uses `gsasl_callback()` or `gsasl_property_get()` to invoke the callback for certain properties.

gsasl_client_callback_authorization_id_get

`Gsasl_client_callback_authorization_id`   [Function]
      `gsasl_client_callback_authorization_id_get` (*Gsasl * ctx*)
   ctx: libgsasl handle.

Get the callback earlier set by calling `gsasl_client_callback_authorization_id_set()`.

Return value: Returns the callback earlier set by calling `gsasl_client_callback_authorization_id_set()`.

Deprecated: This function is part of the old callback interface. The new interface uses `gsasl_callback_set()` to set the application callback, and uses `gsasl_callback()` or `gsasl_property_get()` to invoke the callback for certain properties.

gsasl_client_callback_password_set

`void gsasl_client_callback_password_set` (*Gsasl * ctx*,   [Function]
      Gsasl_client_callback_password cb)
   ctx: libgsasl handle.

   cb: callback function

Specify the callback function to use in the client to set the password. The function can be later retrieved using `gsasl_client_callback_password_get()`.

Deprecated: This function is part of the old callback interface. The new interface uses `gsasl_callback_set()` to set the application callback, and uses `gsasl_callback()` or `gsasl_property_get()` to invoke the callback for certain properties.

gsasl_client_callback_password_get

`Gsasl_client_callback_password`   [Function]
      `gsasl_client_callback_password_get` (*Gsasl * ctx*)
   ctx: libgsasl handle.

Get the callback earlier set by calling `gsasl_client_callback_password_set()`.

Return value: Returns the callback earlier set by calling `gsasl_client_callback_password_set()`.

Deprecated: This function is part of the old callback interface. The new interface uses `gsasl_callback_set()` to set the application callback, and uses `gsasl_callback()` or `gsasl_property_get()` to invoke the callback for certain properties.

gsasl_client_callback_passcode_set

void gsasl_client_callback_passcode_set (*Gsasl* * *ctx*,   [Function]
    Gsasl_client_callback_passcode *cb*)

ctx: libgsasl handle.

cb: callback function

Specify the callback function to use in the client to set the passcode. The function can be later retrieved using `gsasl_client_callback_passcode_get()`.

Deprecated: This function is part of the old callback interface. The new interface uses `gsasl_callback_set()` to set the application callback, and uses `gsasl_callback()` or `gsasl_property_get()` to invoke the callback for certain properties.

gsasl_client_callback_passcode_get

Gsasl_client_callback_passcode   [Function]
    gsasl_client_callback_passcode_get (*Gsasl* * *ctx*)

ctx: libgsasl handle.

Get the callback earlier set by calling `gsasl_client_callback_passcode_set()`.

Return value: Returns the callback earlier set by calling `gsasl_client_callback_passcode_set()`.

Deprecated: This function is part of the old callback interface. The new interface uses `gsasl_callback_set()` to set the application callback, and uses `gsasl_callback()` or `gsasl_property_get()` to invoke the callback for certain properties.

gsasl_client_callback_pin_set

void gsasl_client_callback_pin_set (*Gsasl* * *ctx*,   [Function]
    Gsasl_client_callback_pin *cb*)

ctx: libgsasl handle.

cb: callback function

Specify the callback function to use in the client to chose a new pin, possibly suggested by the server, for the SECURID mechanism. This is not normally invoked, but only when the server requests it. The function can be later retrieved using `gsasl_client_callback_pin_get()`.

Deprecated: This function is part of the old callback interface. The new interface uses `gsasl_callback_set()` to set the application callback, and uses `gsasl_callback()` or `gsasl_property_get()` to invoke the callback for certain properties.

gsasl_client_callback_pin_get

Gsasl_client_callback_pin gsasl_client_callback_pin_get   [Function]
    (*Gsasl* * *ctx*)

ctx: libgsasl handle.

Get the callback earlier set by calling `gsasl_client_callback_pin_set()`.

Return value: Returns the callback earlier set by calling `gsasl_client_callback_pin_set()`.

Deprecated: This function is part of the old callback interface. The new interface uses `gsasl_callback_set()` to set the application callback, and uses `gsasl_callback()` or `gsasl_property_get()` to invoke the callback for certain properties.

gsasl_client_callback_service_set

void gsasl_client_callback_service_set (*Gsasl * ctx*,   [Function]
        Gsasl_client_callback_service cb)
    ctx: libgsasl handle.

    cb: callback function

Specify the callback function to use in the client to set the name of the service. The service buffer should be a registered GSSAPI host-based service name, hostname the name of the server. Servicename is used by DIGEST-MD5 and should be the name of generic server in case of a replicated service. The function can be later retrieved using `gsasl_client_callback_service_get()`.

Deprecated: This function is part of the old callback interface. The new interface uses `gsasl_callback_set()` to set the application callback, and uses `gsasl_callback()` or `gsasl_property_get()` to invoke the callback for certain properties.

gsasl_client_callback_service_get

Gsasl_client_callback_service   [Function]
        gsasl_client_callback_service_get (*Gsasl * ctx*)
    ctx: libgsasl handle.

Get the callback earlier set by calling `gsasl_client_callback_service_set()`.

Return value: Returns the callback earlier set by calling `gsasl_client_callback_service_set()`.

Deprecated: This function is part of the old callback interface. The new interface uses `gsasl_callback_set()` to set the application callback, and uses `gsasl_callback()` or `gsasl_property_get()` to invoke the callback for certain properties.

gsasl_client_callback_anonymous_set

void gsasl_client_callback_anonymous_set (*Gsasl * ctx*,   [Function]
        Gsasl_client_callback_anonymous cb)
    ctx: libgsasl handle.

    cb: callback function

Specify the callback function to use in the client to set the anonymous token, which usually is the users email address. The function can be later retrieved using `gsasl_client_callback_anonymous_get()`.

Deprecated: This function is part of the old callback interface. The new interface uses `gsasl_callback_set()` to set the application callback, and uses `gsasl_callback()` or `gsasl_property_get()` to invoke the callback for certain properties.

gsasl_client_callback_anonymous_get

Gsasl_client_callback_anonymous   [Function]
        gsasl_client_callback_anonymous_get (*Gsasl* * *ctx*)
    ctx: libgsasl handle.

    Get the callback earlier set by calling gsasl_client_callback_anonymous_set().

    Return value: Returns the callback earlier set by calling gsasl_client_callback_anonymous_set().

    Deprecated: This function is part of the old callback interface. The new interface uses gsasl_callback_set() to set the application callback, and uses gsasl_callback() or gsasl_property_get() to invoke the callback for certain properties.

gsasl_client_callback_qop_set

void gsasl_client_callback_qop_set (*Gsasl* * *ctx*,   [Function]
        Gsasl_client_callback_qop *cb*)
    ctx: libgsasl handle.

    cb: callback function

    Specify the callback function to use in the client to determine the qop to use after looking at what the server offered. The function can be later retrieved using gsasl_client_callback_qop_get().

    Deprecated: This function is part of the old callback interface. The new interface uses gsasl_callback_set() to set the application callback, and uses gsasl_callback() or gsasl_property_get() to invoke the callback for certain properties.

gsasl_client_callback_qop_get

Gsasl_client_callback_qop gsasl_client_callback_qop_get   [Function]
        (*Gsasl* * *ctx*)
    ctx: libgsasl handle.

    Get the callback earlier set by calling gsasl_client_callback_qop_set().

    Return value: Returns the callback earlier set by calling gsasl_client_callback_qop_set().

    Deprecated: This function is part of the old callback interface. The new interface uses gsasl_callback_set() to set the application callback, and uses gsasl_callback() or gsasl_property_get() to invoke the callback for certain properties.

gsasl_client_callback_maxbuf_set

void gsasl_client_callback_maxbuf_set (*Gsasl* * *ctx*,   [Function]
        Gsasl_client_callback_maxbuf *cb*)
    ctx: libgsasl handle.

    cb: callback function

    Specify the callback function to use in the client to inform the server of the largest buffer the client is able to receive when using the DIGEST-MD5 "auth-int" or "auth-conf" Quality of Protection (qop). If this directive is missing, the default value 65536 will be assumed. The function can be later retrieved using `gsasl_client_callback_maxbuf_get()`.

Deprecated: This function is part of the old callback interface. The new interface uses `gsasl_callback_set()` to set the application callback, and uses `gsasl_callback()` or `gsasl_property_get()` to invoke the callback for certain properties.

gsasl_client_callback_maxbuf_get

`Gsasl_client_callback_maxbuf` [Function]
     `gsasl_client_callback_maxbuf_get` (*Gsasl* `* ctx`)
    ctx: libgsasl handle.

Get the callback earlier set by calling `gsasl_client_callback_maxbuf_set()`.

Return value: Returns the callback earlier set by calling `gsasl_client_callback_maxbuf_set()`.

Deprecated: This function is part of the old callback interface. The new interface uses `gsasl_callback_set()` to set the application callback, and uses `gsasl_callback()` or `gsasl_property_get()` to invoke the callback for certain properties.

gsasl_client_callback_realm_set

`void gsasl_client_callback_realm_set` (*Gsasl* `* ctx`, [Function]
     Gsasl_client_callback_realm `cb`)
    ctx: libgsasl handle.

    cb: callback function

Specify the callback function to use in the client to know which realm it belongs to. The realm is used by the server to determine which username and password to use. The function can be later retrieved using `gsasl_client_callback_realm_get()`.

Deprecated: This function is part of the old callback interface. The new interface uses `gsasl_callback_set()` to set the application callback, and uses `gsasl_callback()` or `gsasl_property_get()` to invoke the callback for certain properties.

gsasl_client_callback_realm_get

`Gsasl_client_callback_realm` [Function]
     `gsasl_client_callback_realm_get` (*Gsasl* `* ctx`)
    ctx: libgsasl handle.

Get the callback earlier set by calling `gsasl_client_callback_realm_set()`.

Return value: Returns the callback earlier set by calling `gsasl_client_callback_realm_set()`.

Deprecated: This function is part of the old callback interface. The new interface uses `gsasl_callback_set()` to set the application callback, and uses `gsasl_callback()` or `gsasl_property_get()` to invoke the callback for certain properties.

gsasl_server_callback_validate_set

void gsasl_server_callback_validate_set (*Gsasl* * ctx,   [Function]
     Gsasl_server_callback_validate cb)

ctx: libgsasl handle.

cb: callback function

Specify the callback function to use in the server for deciding if user is authenticated using authentication identity, authorization identity and password. The function can be later retrieved using gsasl_server_callback_validate_get().

Deprecated: This function is part of the old callback interface. The new interface uses gsasl_callback_set() to set the application callback, and uses gsasl_callback() or gsasl_property_get() to invoke the callback for certain properties.

gsasl_server_callback_validate_get

Gsasl_server_callback_validate   [Function]
     gsasl_server_callback_validate_get (*Gsasl* * ctx)

ctx: libgsasl handle.

Get the callback earlier set by calling gsasl_server_callback_validate_set().

Return value: Returns the callback earlier set by calling gsasl_server_callback_validate_set().

Deprecated: This function is part of the old callback interface. The new interface uses gsasl_callback_set() to set the application callback, and uses gsasl_callback() or gsasl_property_get() to invoke the callback for certain properties.

gsasl_server_callback_retrieve_set

void gsasl_server_callback_retrieve_set (*Gsasl* * ctx,   [Function]
     Gsasl_server_callback_retrieve cb)

ctx: libgsasl handle.

cb: callback function

Specify the callback function to use in the server for deciding if user is authenticated using authentication identity, authorization identity and password. The function can be later retrieved using gsasl_server_callback_retrieve_get().

Deprecated: This function is part of the old callback interface. The new interface uses gsasl_callback_set() to set the application callback, and uses gsasl_callback() or gsasl_property_get() to invoke the callback for certain properties.

gsasl_server_callback_retrieve_get

Gsasl_server_callback_retrieve   [Function]
     gsasl_server_callback_retrieve_get (*Gsasl* * ctx)

ctx: libgsasl handle.

Get the callback earlier set by calling gsasl_server_callback_retrieve_set().

Return value: Returns the callback earlier set by calling gsasl_server_callback_retrieve_set().

Deprecated: This function is part of the old callback interface. The new interface uses `gsasl_callback_set()` to set the application callback, and uses `gsasl_callback()` or `gsasl_property_get()` to invoke the callback for certain properties.

gsasl_server_callback_cram_md5_set

void gsasl_server_callback_cram_md5_set (*Gsasl* * *ctx*,   [Function]
          Gsasl_server_callback_cram_md5 *cb*)

ctx: libgsasl handle.

cb: callback function

Specify the callback function to use in the server for deciding if user is authenticated using CRAM-MD5 challenge and response. The function can be later retrieved using `gsasl_server_callback_cram_md5_get()`.

Deprecated: This function is part of the old callback interface. The new interface uses `gsasl_callback_set()` to set the application callback, and uses `gsasl_callback()` or `gsasl_property_get()` to invoke the callback for certain properties.

gsasl_server_callback_cram_md5_get

Gsasl_server_callback_cram_md5   [Function]
          gsasl_server_callback_cram_md5_get (*Gsasl* * *ctx*)

ctx: libgsasl handle.

Get the callback earlier set by calling `gsasl_server_callback_cram_md5_set()`.

Return value: Returns the callback earlier set by calling `gsasl_server_callback_cram_md5_set()`.

Deprecated: This function is part of the old callback interface. The new interface uses `gsasl_callback_set()` to set the application callback, and uses `gsasl_callback()` or `gsasl_property_get()` to invoke the callback for certain properties.

gsasl_server_callback_digest_md5_set

void gsasl_server_callback_digest_md5_set (*Gsasl* * *ctx*,   [Function]
          Gsasl_server_callback_digest_md5 *cb*)

ctx: libgsasl handle.

cb: callback function

Specify the callback function to use in the server for retrieving the secret hash of the username, realm and password for use in the DIGEST-MD5 mechanism. The function can be later retrieved using `gsasl_server_callback_digest_md5_get()`.

Deprecated: This function is part of the old callback interface. The new interface uses `gsasl_callback_set()` to set the application callback, and uses `gsasl_callback()` or `gsasl_property_get()` to invoke the callback for certain properties.

gsasl_server_callback_digest_md5_get

Gsasl_server_callback_digest_md5   [Function]
          gsasl_server_callback_digest_md5_get (*Gsasl* * *ctx*)

ctx: libgsasl handle.

Get the callback earlier set by calling `gsasl_server_callback_digest_md5_set()`.

Return value: Return the callback earlier set by calling `gsasl_server_callback_digest_md5_set()`.

Deprecated: This function is part of the old callback interface. The new interface uses `gsasl_callback_set()` to set the application callback, and uses `gsasl_callback()` or `gsasl_property_get()` to invoke the callback for certain properties.

gsasl_server_callback_external_set

void **gsasl_server_callback_external_set** (*Gsasl* * *ctx*,   [Function]
        Gsasl_server_callback_external *cb*)
    ctx: libgsasl handle.

cb: callback function

Specify the callback function to use in the server for deciding if user is authenticated out of band. The function can be later retrieved using `gsasl_server_callback_external_get()`.

Deprecated: This function is part of the old callback interface. The new interface uses `gsasl_callback_set()` to set the application callback, and uses `gsasl_callback()` or `gsasl_property_get()` to invoke the callback for certain properties.

gsasl_server_callback_external_get

Gsasl_server_callback_external   [Function]
        gsasl_server_callback_external_get (*Gsasl* * *ctx*)
    ctx: libgsasl handle.

Get the callback earlier set by calling `gsasl_server_callback_external_set()`.

Return value: Returns the callback earlier set by calling `gsasl_server_callback_external_set()`.

Deprecated: This function is part of the old callback interface. The new interface uses `gsasl_callback_set()` to set the application callback, and uses `gsasl_callback()` or `gsasl_property_get()` to invoke the callback for certain properties.

gsasl_server_callback_anonymous_set

void **gsasl_server_callback_anonymous_set** (*Gsasl* * *ctx*,   [Function]
        Gsasl_server_callback_anonymous *cb*)
    ctx: libgsasl handle.

cb: callback function

Specify the callback function to use in the server for deciding if user is permitted anonymous access. The function can be later retrieved using `gsasl_server_callback_anonymous_get()`.

Deprecated: This function is part of the old callback interface. The new interface uses `gsasl_callback_set()` to set the application callback, and uses `gsasl_callback()` or `gsasl_property_get()` to invoke the callback for certain properties.

gsasl_server_callback_anonymous_get

Gsasl_server_callback_anonymous   [Function]
     gsasl_server_callback_anonymous_get (*Gsasl* * ctx)

ctx: libgsasl handle.

Get the callback earlier set by calling gsasl_server_callback_anonymous_set().

Return value: Returns the callback earlier set by calling gsasl_server_callback_anonymous_set().

Deprecated: This function is part of the old callback interface. The new interface uses gsasl_callback_set() to set the application callback, and uses gsasl_callback() or gsasl_property_get() to invoke the callback for certain properties.

gsasl_server_callback_realm_set

void gsasl_server_callback_realm_set (*Gsasl* * ctx,   [Function]
     Gsasl_server_callback_realm cb)

ctx: libgsasl handle.

cb: callback function

Specify the callback function to use in the server to know which realm it serves. The realm is used by the user to determine which username and password to use. The function can be later retrieved using gsasl_server_callback_realm_get().

Deprecated: This function is part of the old callback interface. The new interface uses gsasl_callback_set() to set the application callback, and uses gsasl_callback() or gsasl_property_get() to invoke the callback for certain properties.

gsasl_server_callback_realm_get

Gsasl_server_callback_realm   [Function]
     gsasl_server_callback_realm_get (*Gsasl* * ctx)

ctx: libgsasl handle.

Get the callback earlier set by calling gsasl_server_callback_realm_set().

Return value: Returns the callback earlier set by calling gsasl_server_callback_realm_set().

Deprecated: This function is part of the old callback interface. The new interface uses gsasl_callback_set() to set the application callback, and uses gsasl_callback() or gsasl_property_get() to invoke the callback for certain properties.

gsasl_server_callback_qop_set

void gsasl_server_callback_qop_set (*Gsasl* * ctx,   [Function]
     Gsasl_server_callback_qop cb)

ctx: libgsasl handle.

cb: callback function

Specify the callback function to use in the server to know which quality of protection it accepts. The quality of protection eventually used is selected by the client though.

It is currently used by the DIGEST-MD5 mechanism. The function can be later retrieved using `gsasl_server_callback_qop_get()`.

Deprecated: This function is part of the old callback interface. The new interface uses `gsasl_callback_set()` to set the application callback, and uses `gsasl_callback()` or `gsasl_property_get()` to invoke the callback for certain properties.

gsasl_server_callback_qop_get

`Gsasl_server_callback_qop gsasl_server_callback_qop_get`   [Function]
    (*Gsasl* * **ctx**)
    ctx: libgsasl handle.

Get the callback earlier set by calling `gsasl_server_callback_qop_set()`.

Return value: Returns the callback earlier set by calling `gsasl_server_callback_qop_set()`.

Deprecated: This function is part of the old callback interface. The new interface uses `gsasl_callback_set()` to set the application callback, and uses `gsasl_callback()` or `gsasl_property_get()` to invoke the callback for certain properties.

gsasl_server_callback_maxbuf_set

`void gsasl_server_callback_maxbuf_set` (*Gsasl* * **ctx**,   [Function]
    Gsasl_server_callback_maxbuf **cb**)
    ctx: libgsasl handle.

    cb: callback function

Specify the callback function to use in the server to inform the client of the largest buffer the server is able to receive when using the DIGEST-MD5 "auth-int" or "auth-conf" Quality of Protection (qop). If this directive is missing, the default value 65536 will be assumed. The function can be later retrieved using `gsasl_server_callback_maxbuf_get()`.

Deprecated: This function is part of the old callback interface. The new interface uses `gsasl_callback_set()` to set the application callback, and uses `gsasl_callback()` or `gsasl_property_get()` to invoke the callback for certain properties.

gsasl_server_callback_maxbuf_get

`Gsasl_server_callback_maxbuf`   [Function]
    `gsasl_server_callback_maxbuf_get` (*Gsasl* * **ctx**)
    ctx: libgsasl handle.

Get the callback earlier set by calling `gsasl_server_callback_maxbuf_set()`.

Return value: Returns the callback earlier set by calling `gsasl_server_callback_maxbuf_set()`.

Deprecated: This function is part of the old callback interface. The new interface uses `gsasl_callback_set()` to set the application callback, and uses `gsasl_callback()` or `gsasl_property_get()` to invoke the callback for certain properties.

gsasl_server_callback_cipher_set

void gsasl_server_callback_cipher_set (*Gsasl * ctx*,   [Function]
        Gsasl_server_callback_cipher cb)

ctx: libgsasl handle.

cb: callback function

Specify the callback function to use in the server to inform the client of the cipher suites supported. The DES and 3DES ciphers must be supported for interoperability. It is currently used by the DIGEST-MD5 mechanism. The function can be later retrieved using gsasl_server_callback_cipher_get().

Deprecated: This function is part of the old callback interface. The new interface uses gsasl_callback_set() to set the application callback, and uses gsasl_callback() or gsasl_property_get() to invoke the callback for certain properties.

gsasl_server_callback_cipher_get

Gsasl_server_callback_cipher   [Function]
        gsasl_server_callback_cipher_get (*Gsasl * ctx*)

ctx: libgsasl handle.

Get the callback earlier set by calling gsasl_server_callback_cipher_set().

Return value: Returns the callback earlier set by calling gsasl_server_callback_cipher_set().

Deprecated: This function is part of the old callback interface. The new interface uses gsasl_callback_set() to set the application callback, and uses gsasl_callback() or gsasl_property_get() to invoke the callback for certain properties.

gsasl_server_callback_securid_set

void gsasl_server_callback_securid_set (*Gsasl * ctx*,   [Function]
        Gsasl_server_callback_securid cb)

ctx: libgsasl handle.

cb: callback function

Specify the callback function to use in the server for validating a user via the SECURID mechanism. The function should return GSASL_OK if user authenticated successfully, GSASL_SECURID_SERVER_NEED_ADDITIONAL_PASSCODE if it wants another passcode, GSASL_SECURID_SERVER_NEED_NEW_PIN if it wants a PIN change, or an error. When (and only when) GSASL_SECURID_SERVER_NEED_NEW_PIN is returned, suggestpin can be populated with a PIN code the server suggests, and suggestpinlen set to the length of the PIN. The function can be later retrieved using gsasl_server_callback_securid_get().

Deprecated: This function is part of the old callback interface. The new interface uses gsasl_callback_set() to set the application callback, and uses gsasl_callback() or gsasl_property_get() to invoke the callback for certain properties.

gsasl_server_callback_securid_get

Gsasl_server_callback_securid   [Function]
    gsasl_server_callback_securid_get (*Gsasl* * *ctx*)

ctx: libgsasl handle.

Get the callback earlier set by calling `gsasl_server_callback_securid_set()`.

Return value: Returns the callback earlier set by calling `gsasl_server_callback_securid_set()`.

Deprecated: This function is part of the old callback interface. The new interface uses `gsasl_callback_set()` to set the application callback, and uses `gsasl_callback()` or `gsasl_property_get()` to invoke the callback for certain properties.

gsasl_server_callback_gssapi_set

void gsasl_server_callback_gssapi_set (*Gsasl* * *ctx*,   [Function]
    Gsasl_server_callback_gssapi cb)

ctx: libgsasl handle.

cb: callback function

Specify the callback function to use in the server for checking if a GSSAPI user is authorized for username (by, e.g., calling krb5_kuserok). The function should return GSASL_OK if the user should be permitted access, or an error code such as GSASL_AUTHENTICATION_ERROR on failure. The function can be later retrieved using `gsasl_server_callback_gssapi_get()`.

Deprecated: This function is part of the old callback interface. The new interface uses `gsasl_callback_set()` to set the application callback, and uses `gsasl_callback()` or `gsasl_property_get()` to invoke the callback for certain properties.

gsasl_server_callback_gssapi_get

Gsasl_server_callback_gssapi   [Function]
    gsasl_server_callback_gssapi_get (*Gsasl* * *ctx*)

ctx: libgsasl handle.

Get the callback earlier set by calling `gsasl_server_callback_gssapi_set()`.

Return value: Returns the callback earlier set by calling `gsasl_server_callback_gssapi_set()`.

Deprecated: This function is part of the old callback interface. The new interface uses `gsasl_callback_set()` to set the application callback, and uses `gsasl_callback()` or `gsasl_property_get()` to invoke the callback for certain properties.

gsasl_server_callback_service_set

void gsasl_server_callback_service_set (*Gsasl* * *ctx*,   [Function]
    Gsasl_server_callback_service cb)

ctx: libgsasl handle.

cb: callback function

Specify the callback function to use in the server to set the name of the service. The service buffer should be a registered GSSAPI host-based service name, hostname the name of the server. The function can be later retrieved using `gsasl_server_callback_service_get()`.

Deprecated: This function is part of the old callback interface. The new interface uses `gsasl_callback_set()` to set the application callback, and uses `gsasl_callback()` or `gsasl_property_get()` to invoke the callback for certain properties.

gsasl_server_callback_service_get

`Gsasl_server_callback_service`   [Function]
    `gsasl_server_callback_service_get` (*Gsasl * ctx*)
ctx: libgsasl handle.

Get the callback earlier set by calling `gsasl_server_callback_service_set()`.

Return value: Returns the callback earlier set by calling `gsasl_server_callback_service_set()`.

Deprecated: This function is part of the old callback interface. The new interface uses `gsasl_callback_set()` to set the application callback, and uses `gsasl_callback()` or `gsasl_property_get()` to invoke the callback for certain properties.

gsasl_stringprep_nfkc

`char * gsasl_stringprep_nfkc` (*const char * in, ssize_t len*)   [Function]
    in: a UTF-8 encoded string.

    len: length of `str`, in bytes, or -1 if `str` is nul-terminated.

    Converts a string into canonical form, standardizing such issues as whether a character with an accent is represented as a base character and combining accent or as a single precomposed character.

    The normalization mode is NFKC (ALL COMPOSE). It standardizes differences that do not affect the text content, such as the above-mentioned accent representation. It standardizes the "compatibility" characters in Unicode, such as SUPERSCRIPT THREE to the standard forms (in this case DIGIT THREE). Formatting information may be lost but for most text operations such characters should be considered the same. It returns a result with composed forms rather than a maximally decomposed form.

    Return value: Return a newly allocated string, that is the NFKC normalized form of `str`, or NULL on error.

    Deprecated: No replacement functionality in GNU SASL, use GNU Libidn instead. Note that in SASL, you most likely want to use SASLprep and not bare NFKC, see `gsasl_saslprep()`.

gsasl_stringprep_saslprep

`char * gsasl_stringprep_saslprep` (*const char * in, int **   [Function]
    stringprep_rc)
    in: input ASCII or UTF-8 string with data to prepare according to SASLprep.

stringprep_rc: pointer to output variable with stringprep error code, or NULL to indicate that you don't care about it.

Process a Unicode string for comparison, according to the "SASLprep" stringprep profile. This function is intended to be used by Simple Authentication and Security Layer (SASL) mechanisms (such as PLAIN, CRAM-MD5, and DIGEST-MD5) as well as other protocols exchanging user names and/or passwords.

Return value: Return a newly allocated string that is the "SASLprep" processed form of the input string, or NULL on error, in which case `stringprep_rc` contain the stringprep library error code.

Deprecated: Use `gsasl_saslprep()` instead.

gsasl_stringprep_trace

`char * gsasl_stringprep_trace` (*const char * in*, *int **   [Function]
       stringprep_rc)

in: input ASCII or UTF-8 string with data to prepare according to "trace".

stringprep_rc: pointer to output variable with stringprep error code, or NULL to indicate that you don't care about it.

Process a Unicode string for use as trace information, according to the "trace" stringprep profile. The profile is designed for use with the SASL ANONYMOUS Mechanism.

Return value: Return a newly allocated string that is the "trace" processed form of the input string, or NULL on error, in which case `stringprep_rc` contain the stringprep library error code.

Deprecated: No replacement functionality in GNU SASL, use GNU Libidn instead.

gsasl_md5pwd_get_password

`int gsasl_md5pwd_get_password` (*const char * filename*, *const char*   [Function]
       * username, *char * key*, *size_t * keylen*)

filename: filename of file containing passwords.

username: username string.

key: output character array.

keylen: input maximum size of output character array, on output contains actual length of output array.

Retrieve password for user from specified file. To find out how large the output array must be, call this function with out=NULL.

The file should be on the UoW "MD5 Based Authentication" format, which means it is in text format with comments denoted by # first on the line, with user entries looking as "usernameTABpassword". This function removes CR and LF at the end of lines before processing. TAB, CR, and LF denote ASCII values 9, 13, and 10, respectively.

Return value: Return GSASL_OK if output buffer contains the password, GSASL_AUTHENTICATION_ERROR if the user could not be found, or other error code.

Deprecated: Use `gsasl_simple_getpass()` instead.

gsasl_base64_encode

int gsasl_base64_encode (*char const* * **src**, *size_t* **srclength**, *char* *   [Function]
       target, *size_t* **targsize**)

    src: input byte array

    srclength: size of input byte array

    target: output byte array

    targsize: size of output byte array

    Encode data as base64. Converts characters, three at a time, starting at src into four base64 characters in the target area until the entire input buffer is encoded.

    Return value: Returns the number of data bytes stored at the target, or -1 on error.

    Deprecated: Use `gsasl_base64_to()` instead.

gsasl_base64_decode

int gsasl_base64_decode (*char const* * **src**, *char* * **target**, *size_t*   [Function]
       targsize)

    src: input byte array

    target: output byte array

    targsize: size of output byte array

    Decode Base64 data. Skips all whitespace anywhere. Converts characters, four at a time, starting at (or after) src from Base64 numbers into three 8 bit bytes in the target area.

    Return value: Returns the number of data bytes stored at the target, or -1 on error.

    Deprecated: Use `gsasl_base64_from()` instead.

B.1 Obsolete callback function prototypes

int (*Gsasl_client_callback_anonymous) (*Gsasl_session_ctx* *   [Prototype]
       ctx, *char* * **out**, *size_t* * **outlen**)

    ctx: libgsasl handle.

    out: output array with client token.

    outlen: on input the maximum size of the output array, on output contains the actual size of the output array.

    Type of callback function the application implements. It should populate the output array with some input from the user and set the output array length, and return `GSASL_OK`, or fail with an error code.

    If OUT is NULL, the function should only populate the output length field with the length, and return GSASL_OK. This usage may be used by the caller to allocate the proper buffer size.

int (*Gsasl_server_callback_anonymous) (*Gsasl_session_ctx* *   [Prototype]
       ctx, *const char* * **token**)

    ctx: libgsasl handle.

ctx: output array with client token.

ctx: on input the maximum size of the output array, on output contains the actual size of the output array. If OUT is

Type of callback function the application implements. It should return `GSASL_OK` if user should be permitted anonymous access, otherwise `GSASL_AUTHENTICATION_ERROR`.

int (*Gsasl_client_callback_authentication_id)   [Prototype]
    (*Gsasl_session_ctx* * **ctx**, *char* * **out**, *size_t* * **outlen**)
ctx: libgsasl handle.

out: output array with authentication identity.

outlen: on input the maximum size of the output array, on output contains the actual size of the output array.

Type of callback function the application implements. It should populate the output array with authentiction identity of user and set the output array length, and return `GSASL_OK`, or fail with an error code. The authentication identity must be encoded in UTF-8, but need not be normalized in any way.

If OUT is NULL, the function should only populate the output length field with the length, and return GSASL_OK. This usage may be used by the caller to allocate the proper buffer size.

int (*Gsasl_client_callback_authorization_id)   [Prototype]
    (*Gsasl_session_ctx* * **ctx**, *char* * **out**, *size_t* * **outlen**)
ctx: libgsasl handle.

out: output array with authorization identity.

outlen: on input the maximum size of the output array, on output contains the actual size of the output array.

Type of callback function the application implements. It should populate the output array with authorization identity of user and set the output array length, and return `GSASL_OK`, or fail with an error code. The authorization identity must be encoded in UTF-8, but need not be normalized in any way.

If OUT is NULL, the function should only populate the output length field with the length, and return GSASL_OK. This usage may be used by the caller to allocate the proper buffer size.

int (*Gsasl_client_callback_service) (*Gsasl_session_ctx* * **ctx**,   [Prototype]
    char * **service**, *size_t* * **servicelen**, *char* * **hostname**, *size_t* *
    hostnamelen, *char* * **servicename**, *size_t* * **servicenamelen**)
ctx: libgsasl handle.

service: output array with name of service.

servicelen: on input the maximum size of the service output array, on output contains the actual size of the service output array.

hostname: output array with hostname of server.

hostnamelen: on input the maximum size of the hostname output array, on output contains the actual size of the hostname output array.

servicename: output array with generic name of server in case of replication (DIGEST-MD5 only).

servicenamelen: on input the maximum size of the servicename output array, on output contains the actual size of the servicename output array.

Type of callback function the application implements. It should retrieve the service (which should be a registered GSSAPI host based service name, such as "imap") on the server, hostname of server (usually canoncial DNS hostname) and optionally generic service name of server in case of replication (e.g. "mail.example.org" when the hostname is "mx42.example.org", see the RFC 2831 for more information). It should return GSASL_OK, or an error such as GSASL_AUTHENTICATION_ERROR if it fails.

If SERVICE, HOSTNAME or SERVICENAME is NULL, the function should only populate SERVICELEN, HOSTNAMELEN or SERVICENAMELEN with the output length of the respective field, and return GSASL_OK. This usage may be used by the caller to allocate the proper buffer size. Furthermore, SERVICENAMELEN may also be NULL, indicating that the mechanism is not interested in this field.

int (*Gsasl_server_callback_cram_md5) (*Gsasl_session_ctx* * ctx,   [Prototype]
    char * username, *char* * challenge, *char* * response)

ctx: libgsasl handle.

username: input array with username.

challenge: input array with CRAM-MD5 challenge.

response: input array with CRAM-MD5 response.

Type of callback function the application implements. It should return GSASL_OK if and only if the validation of the provided credential was succesful. GSASL_AUTHENTICATION_ERROR is a good failure if authentication failed, but any available return code may be used.

int (*Gsasl_server_callback_digest_md5) (*Gsasl_session_ctx* *   [Prototype]
    ctx, *char* * username, *char* * realm, *char* * secrethash)

ctx: libgsasl handle.

username: input array with authentication identity of user.

realm: input array with realm of user.

secrethash: output array that should contain hash of username, realm and password as described for the DIGEST-MD5 mechanism.

Type of callback function the application implements. It should retrieve the secret hash for the given user in given realm and return GSASL_OK, or an error such as GSASL_AUTHENTICATION_ERROR if it fails. The secrethash buffer is guaranteed to have size for the fixed length MD5 hash.

int (*Gsasl_server_callback_external) (*Gsasl_session_ctx* *   [Prototype]
    ctx)

ctx: libgsasl handle.

Type of callback function the application implements. It should return `GSASL_OK` if user is authenticated by out of band means, otherwise `GSASL_AUTHENTICATION_ ERROR`.

int (*Gsasl_server_callback_gssapi) (*Gsasl_session_ctx* * **ctx**,   [Prototype]
    char * **clientname**, *char* * **authentication_id**)
    ctx: libgsasl handle.

clientname: input array with GSSAPI client name.

authentication_id: input array with authentication identity.

Type of callback function the application implements. It should return GSASL_OK
if and only if the GSSAPI user is authorized to log on as the given authentication_id.
GSASL_AUTHENTICATION_ERROR is a good failure if authentication failed, but
any available return code may be used. This callback is usually implemented in the
application as a call to krb5_kuserok(), such as:

```
int
callback_gssapi (Gsasl_session_ctx *ctx,
 char *clientname,
 char *authentication_id)
{
  int rc = GSASL_AUTHENTICATION_ERROR;

  krb5_principal p;
  krb5_context kcontext;

  krb5_init_context (&kcontext);

  if (krb5_parse_name (kcontext, clientname, &p) != 0)
    return -1;
  if (krb5_kuserok (kcontext, p, authentication_id))
    rc = GSASL_OK;
  krb5_free_principal (kcontext, p);

  return rc;
}
```

int (*Gsasl_client_callback_passcode) (*Gsasl_session_ctx* * **ctx**,   [Prototype]
    char * **out**, *size_t* * **outlen**)
    ctx: libgsasl handle.

out: output array with passcode.

outlen: on input the maximum size of the output array, on output contains the actual
size of the output array.

Type of callback function the application implements. It should populate the output
array with passcode of user and set the output array length, and return `GSASL_OK`,
or fail with an error code.

If OUT is NULL, the function should only populate the output length field with the
length, and return GSASL_OK. This usage may be used by the caller to allocate the
proper buffer size.

int (*Gsasl_client_callback_password) (*Gsasl_session_ctx* * ctx,   [Prototype]
        char * out, *size_t* * outlen)

ctx: libgsasl handle.

out: output array with password.

outlen: on input the maximum size of the output array, on output contains the actual size of the output array.

Type of callback function the application implements. It should populate the output array with password of user and set the output array length, and return GSASL_OK, or fail with an error code. The password must be encoded in UTF-8, but need not be normalized in any way.

If OUT is NULL, the function should only populate the output length field with the length, and return GSASL_OK. This usage may be used by the caller to allocate the proper buffer size.

int (*Gsasl_server_callback_retrieve) (*Gsasl_session_ctx* * ctx,   [Prototype]
        char * authentication_id, *char* * authorization_id, *char* * realm, *char*
        * key, *size_t* * keylen)

ctx: libgsasl handle.

authentication_id: input array with authentication identity.

authorization_id: input array with authorization identity, or NULL.

realm: input array with realm of user, or NULL.

key: output array with key for authentication identity.

keylen: on input the maximum size of the key output array, on output contains the actual size of the key output array.

Type of callback function the application implements. It should retrieve the password for the indicated user and return GSASL_OK, or an error code such as GSASL_AUTHENTICATION_ERROR. The key must be encoded in UTF-8, but need not be normalized in any way.

If KEY is NULL, the function should only populate the KEYLEN output length field with the length, and return GSASL_OK. This usage may be used by the caller to allocate the proper buffer size.

int (*Gsasl_server_callback_validate) (*Gsasl_session_ctx* * ctx,   [Prototype]
        char * authentication_id, *char* * authorization_id, *char* * passcode,
        char * pin, *char* * suggestpin, *size_t* * suggestpinlen)

ctx: libgsasl handle.

authorization_id: input array with authorization identity.

authentication_id: input array with authentication identity.

passcode: input array with passcode.

pin: input array with new pin (this may be NULL).

suggestpin: output array with new suggested PIN.

suggestpinlen: on input the maximum size of the output array, on output contains the actual size of the output array.

Type of callback function the application implements. It should return GSASL_OK if and only if the validation of the provided credential was succesful. GSASL_AUTHENTICATION_ERROR is a good failure if authentication failed, but any available return code may be used.

Two SECURID specific error codes also exists. The function can return GSASL_SECURID_SERVER_NEED_ADDITIONAL_PASSCODE to request that the client generate a new passcode. It can also return GSASL_SECURID_SERVER_NEED_NEW_PIN to request that the client generate a new PIN. If the server wishes to suggest a new PIN it can populate the SUGGESTPIN field.

If SUGGESTPIN is NULL, the function should only populate the output length field with the length, and return GSASL_OK. This usage may be used by the caller to allocate the proper buffer size.

int (*Gsasl_server_callback_service) (*Gsasl_session_ctx* * ctx*,   [Prototype]
    char * service*, *size_t* * servicelen*, *char* * hostname*, *size_t* *
    hostnamelen*)

ctx: libgsasl handle.

service: output array with name of service.

servicelen: on input the maximum size of the service output array, on output contains the actual size of the service output array.

hostname: output array with hostname of server.

hostnamelen: on input the maximum size of the hostname output array, on output contains the actual size of the hostname output array.

Type of callback function the application implements. It should retrieve the service (which should be a registered GSSAPI host based service name, such as "imap") the server provides and hostname of server (usually canoncial DNS hostname). It should return GSASL_OK, or an error such as GSASL_AUTHENTICATION_ERROR if it fails.

If SERVICE or HOSTNAME is NULL, the function should only populate SERVICE-LEN or HOSTNAMELEN with the output length of the respective field, and return GSASL_OK. This usage may be used by the caller to allocate the proper buffer size.

int (*Gsasl_server_callback_validate) (*Gsasl_session_ctx* * ctx*,   [Prototype]
    char * authorization_id*, *char* * authentication_id*, *char* * password*)

ctx: libgsasl handle.

authorization_id: input array with authorization identity.

authentication_id: input array with authentication identity.

password: input array with password.

Type of callback function the application implements. It should return GSASL_OK if and only if the validation of the provided credential was succesful. GSASL_AUTHENTICATION_ERROR is a good failure if authentication failed, but any available return code may be used.

Appendix C Copying Information

C.1 GNU Free Documentation License

Version 1.3, 3 November 2008

Copyright © 2000, 2001, 2002, 2007, 2008 Free Software Foundation, Inc.
`http://fsf.org/`

Everyone is permitted to copy and distribute verbatim copies
of this license document, but changing it is not allowed.

0. PREAMBLE

The purpose of this License is to make a manual, textbook, or other functional and useful document *free* in the sense of freedom: to assure everyone the effective freedom to copy and redistribute it, with or without modifying it, either commercially or non-commercially. Secondarily, this License preserves for the author and publisher a way to get credit for their work, while not being considered responsible for modifications made by others.

This License is a kind of "copyleft", which means that derivative works of the document must themselves be free in the same sense. It complements the GNU General Public License, which is a copyleft license designed for free software.

We have designed this License in order to use it for manuals for free software, because free software needs free documentation: a free program should come with manuals providing the same freedoms that the software does. But this License is not limited to software manuals; it can be used for any textual work, regardless of subject matter or whether it is published as a printed book. We recommend this License principally for works whose purpose is instruction or reference.

1. APPLICABILITY AND DEFINITIONS

This License applies to any manual or other work, in any medium, that contains a notice placed by the copyright holder saying it can be distributed under the terms of this License. Such a notice grants a world-wide, royalty-free license, unlimited in duration, to use that work under the conditions stated herein. The "Document", below, refers to any such manual or work. Any member of the public is a licensee, and is addressed as "you". You accept the license if you copy, modify or distribute the work in a way requiring permission under copyright law.

A "Modified Version" of the Document means any work containing the Document or a portion of it, either copied verbatim, or with modifications and/or translated into another language.

A "Secondary Section" is a named appendix or a front-matter section of the Document that deals exclusively with the relationship of the publishers or authors of the Document to the Document's overall subject (or to related matters) and contains nothing that could fall directly within that overall subject. (Thus, if the Document is in part a textbook of mathematics, a Secondary Section may not explain any mathematics.) The relationship could be a matter of historical connection with the subject or with related matters, or of legal, commercial, philosophical, ethical or political position regarding them.

The "Invariant Sections" are certain Secondary Sections whose titles are designated, as being those of Invariant Sections, in the notice that says that the Document is released under this License. If a section does not fit the above definition of Secondary then it is not allowed to be designated as Invariant. The Document may contain zero Invariant Sections. If the Document does not identify any Invariant Sections then there are none.

The "Cover Texts" are certain short passages of text that are listed, as Front-Cover Texts or Back-Cover Texts, in the notice that says that the Document is released under this License. A Front-Cover Text may be at most 5 words, and a Back-Cover Text may be at most 25 words.

A "Transparent" copy of the Document means a machine-readable copy, represented in a format whose specification is available to the general public, that is suitable for revising the document straightforwardly with generic text editors or (for images composed of pixels) generic paint programs or (for drawings) some widely available drawing editor, and that is suitable for input to text formatters or for automatic translation to a variety of formats suitable for input to text formatters. A copy made in an otherwise Transparent file format whose markup, or absence of markup, has been arranged to thwart or discourage subsequent modification by readers is not Transparent. An image format is not Transparent if used for any substantial amount of text. A copy that is not "Transparent" is called "Opaque".

Examples of suitable formats for Transparent copies include plain ASCII without markup, Texinfo input format, LaTeX input format, SGML or XML using a publicly available DTD, and standard-conforming simple HTML, PostScript or PDF designed for human modification. Examples of transparent image formats include PNG, XCF and JPG. Opaque formats include proprietary formats that can be read and edited only by proprietary word processors, SGML or XML for which the DTD and/or processing tools are not generally available, and the machine-generated HTML, PostScript or PDF produced by some word processors for output purposes only.

The "Title Page" means, for a printed book, the title page itself, plus such following pages as are needed to hold, legibly, the material this License requires to appear in the title page. For works in formats which do not have any title page as such, "Title Page" means the text near the most prominent appearance of the work's title, preceding the beginning of the body of the text.

The "publisher" means any person or entity that distributes copies of the Document to the public.

A section "Entitled XYZ" means a named subunit of the Document whose title either is precisely XYZ or contains XYZ in parentheses following text that translates XYZ in another language. (Here XYZ stands for a specific section name mentioned below, such as "Acknowledgements", "Dedications", "Endorsements", or "History".) To "Preserve the Title" of such a section when you modify the Document means that it remains a section "Entitled XYZ" according to this definition.

The Document may include Warranty Disclaimers next to the notice which states that this License applies to the Document. These Warranty Disclaimers are considered to be included by reference in this License, but only as regards disclaiming warranties: any other implication that these Warranty Disclaimers may have is void and has no effect on the meaning of this License.

2. VERBATIM COPYING

You may copy and distribute the Document in any medium, either commercially or noncommercially, provided that this License, the copyright notices, and the license notice saying this License applies to the Document are reproduced in all copies, and that you add no other conditions whatsoever to those of this License. You may not use technical measures to obstruct or control the reading or further copying of the copies you make or distribute. However, you may accept compensation in exchange for copies. If you distribute a large enough number of copies you must also follow the conditions in section 3.

You may also lend copies, under the same conditions stated above, and you may publicly display copies.

3. COPYING IN QUANTITY

If you publish printed copies (or copies in media that commonly have printed covers) of the Document, numbering more than 100, and the Document's license notice requires Cover Texts, you must enclose the copies in covers that carry, clearly and legibly, all these Cover Texts: Front-Cover Texts on the front cover, and Back-Cover Texts on the back cover. Both covers must also clearly and legibly identify you as the publisher of these copies. The front cover must present the full title with all words of the title equally prominent and visible. You may add other material on the covers in addition. Copying with changes limited to the covers, as long as they preserve the title of the Document and satisfy these conditions, can be treated as verbatim copying in other respects.

If the required texts for either cover are too voluminous to fit legibly, you should put the first ones listed (as many as fit reasonably) on the actual cover, and continue the rest onto adjacent pages.

If you publish or distribute Opaque copies of the Document numbering more than 100, you must either include a machine-readable Transparent copy along with each Opaque copy, or state in or with each Opaque copy a computer-network location from which the general network-using public has access to download using public-standard network protocols a complete Transparent copy of the Document, free of added material. If you use the latter option, you must take reasonably prudent steps, when you begin distribution of Opaque copies in quantity, to ensure that this Transparent copy will remain thus accessible at the stated location until at least one year after the last time you distribute an Opaque copy (directly or through your agents or retailers) of that edition to the public.

It is requested, but not required, that you contact the authors of the Document well before redistributing any large number of copies, to give them a chance to provide you with an updated version of the Document.

4. MODIFICATIONS

You may copy and distribute a Modified Version of the Document under the conditions of sections 2 and 3 above, provided that you release the Modified Version under precisely this License, with the Modified Version filling the role of the Document, thus licensing distribution and modification of the Modified Version to whoever possesses a copy of it. In addition, you must do these things in the Modified Version:

A. Use in the Title Page (and on the covers, if any) a title distinct from that of the Document, and from those of previous versions (which should, if there were any, be listed in the History section of the Document). You may use the same title as a previous version if the original publisher of that version gives permission.

B. List on the Title Page, as authors, one or more persons or entities responsible for authorship of the modifications in the Modified Version, together with at least five of the principal authors of the Document (all of its principal authors, if it has fewer than five), unless they release you from this requirement.

C. State on the Title page the name of the publisher of the Modified Version, as the publisher.

D. Preserve all the copyright notices of the Document.

E. Add an appropriate copyright notice for your modifications adjacent to the other copyright notices.

F. Include, immediately after the copyright notices, a license notice giving the public permission to use the Modified Version under the terms of this License, in the form shown in the Addendum below.

G. Preserve in that license notice the full lists of Invariant Sections and required Cover Texts given in the Document's license notice.

H. Include an unaltered copy of this License.

I. Preserve the section Entitled "History", Preserve its Title, and add to it an item stating at least the title, year, new authors, and publisher of the Modified Version as given on the Title Page. If there is no section Entitled "History" in the Document, create one stating the title, year, authors, and publisher of the Document as given on its Title Page, then add an item describing the Modified Version as stated in the previous sentence.

J. Preserve the network location, if any, given in the Document for public access to a Transparent copy of the Document, and likewise the network locations given in the Document for previous versions it was based on. These may be placed in the "History" section. You may omit a network location for a work that was published at least four years before the Document itself, or if the original publisher of the version it refers to gives permission.

K. For any section Entitled "Acknowledgements" or "Dedications", Preserve the Title of the section, and preserve in the section all the substance and tone of each of the contributor acknowledgements and/or dedications given therein.

L. Preserve all the Invariant Sections of the Document, unaltered in their text and in their titles. Section numbers or the equivalent are not considered part of the section titles.

M. Delete any section Entitled "Endorsements". Such a section may not be included in the Modified Version.

N. Do not retitle any existing section to be Entitled "Endorsements" or to conflict in title with any Invariant Section.

O. Preserve any Warranty Disclaimers.

If the Modified Version includes new front-matter sections or appendices that qualify as Secondary Sections and contain no material copied from the Document, you may at your option designate some or all of these sections as invariant. To do this, add their titles to the list of Invariant Sections in the Modified Version's license notice. These titles must be distinct from any other section titles.

You may add a section Entitled "Endorsements", provided it contains nothing but endorsements of your Modified Version by various parties—for example, statements of peer review or that the text has been approved by an organization as the authoritative definition of a standard.

You may add a passage of up to five words as a Front-Cover Text, and a passage of up to 25 words as a Back-Cover Text, to the end of the list of Cover Texts in the Modified Version. Only one passage of Front-Cover Text and one of Back-Cover Text may be added by (or through arrangements made by) any one entity. If the Document already includes a cover text for the same cover, previously added by you or by arrangement made by the same entity you are acting on behalf of, you may not add another; but you may replace the old one, on explicit permission from the previous publisher that added the old one.

The author(s) and publisher(s) of the Document do not by this License give permission to use their names for publicity for or to assert or imply endorsement of any Modified Version.

5. COMBINING DOCUMENTS

You may combine the Document with other documents released under this License, under the terms defined in section 4 above for modified versions, provided that you include in the combination all of the Invariant Sections of all of the original documents, unmodified, and list them all as Invariant Sections of your combined work in its license notice, and that you preserve all their Warranty Disclaimers.

The combined work need only contain one copy of this License, and multiple identical Invariant Sections may be replaced with a single copy. If there are multiple Invariant Sections with the same name but different contents, make the title of each such section unique by adding at the end of it, in parentheses, the name of the original author or publisher of that section if known, or else a unique number. Make the same adjustment to the section titles in the list of Invariant Sections in the license notice of the combined work.

In the combination, you must combine any sections Entitled "History" in the various original documents, forming one section Entitled "History"; likewise combine any sections Entitled "Acknowledgements", and any sections Entitled "Dedications". You must delete all sections Entitled "Endorsements."

6. COLLECTIONS OF DOCUMENTS

You may make a collection consisting of the Document and other documents released under this License, and replace the individual copies of this License in the various documents with a single copy that is included in the collection, provided that you follow the rules of this License for verbatim copying of each of the documents in all other respects.

You may extract a single document from such a collection, and distribute it individually under this License, provided you insert a copy of this License into the extracted document, and follow this License in all other respects regarding verbatim copying of that document.

7. AGGREGATION WITH INDEPENDENT WORKS

A compilation of the Document or its derivatives with other separate and independent documents or works, in or on a volume of a storage or distribution medium, is called an "aggregate" if the copyright resulting from the compilation is not used to limit the legal rights of the compilation's users beyond what the individual works permit. When the Document is included in an aggregate, this License does not apply to the other works in the aggregate which are not themselves derivative works of the Document.

If the Cover Text requirement of section 3 is applicable to these copies of the Document, then if the Document is less than one half of the entire aggregate, the Document's Cover Texts may be placed on covers that bracket the Document within the aggregate, or the electronic equivalent of covers if the Document is in electronic form. Otherwise they must appear on printed covers that bracket the whole aggregate.

8. TRANSLATION

Translation is considered a kind of modification, so you may distribute translations of the Document under the terms of section 4. Replacing Invariant Sections with translations requires special permission from their copyright holders, but you may include translations of some or all Invariant Sections in addition to the original versions of these Invariant Sections. You may include a translation of this License, and all the license notices in the Document, and any Warranty Disclaimers, provided that you also include the original English version of this License and the original versions of those notices and disclaimers. In case of a disagreement between the translation and the original version of this License or a notice or disclaimer, the original version will prevail.

If a section in the Document is Entitled "Acknowledgements", "Dedications", or "History", the requirement (section 4) to Preserve its Title (section 1) will typically require changing the actual title.

9. TERMINATION

You may not copy, modify, sublicense, or distribute the Document except as expressly provided under this License. Any attempt otherwise to copy, modify, sublicense, or distribute it is void, and will automatically terminate your rights under this License.

However, if you cease all violation of this License, then your license from a particular copyright holder is reinstated (a) provisionally, unless and until the copyright holder explicitly and finally terminates your license, and (b) permanently, if the copyright holder fails to notify you of the violation by some reasonable means prior to 60 days after the cessation.

Moreover, your license from a particular copyright holder is reinstated permanently if the copyright holder notifies you of the violation by some reasonable means, this is the first time you have received notice of violation of this License (for any work) from that copyright holder, and you cure the violation prior to 30 days after your receipt of the notice.

Termination of your rights under this section does not terminate the licenses of parties who have received copies or rights from you under this License. If your rights have been terminated and not permanently reinstated, receipt of a copy of some or all of the same material does not give you any rights to use it.

10. FUTURE REVISIONS OF THIS LICENSE

The Free Software Foundation may publish new, revised versions of the GNU Free Documentation License from time to time. Such new versions will be similar in spirit to the present version, but may differ in detail to address new problems or concerns. See http://www.gnu.org/copyleft/.

Each version of the License is given a distinguishing version number. If the Document specifies that a particular numbered version of this License "or any later version" applies to it, you have the option of following the terms and conditions either of that specified version or of any later version that has been published (not as a draft) by the Free Software Foundation. If the Document does not specify a version number of this License, you may choose any version ever published (not as a draft) by the Free Software Foundation. If the Document specifies that a proxy can decide which future versions of this License can be used, that proxy's public statement of acceptance of a version permanently authorizes you to choose that version for the Document.

11. RELICENSING

"Massive Multiauthor Collaboration Site" (or "MMC Site") means any World Wide Web server that publishes copyrightable works and also provides prominent facilities for anybody to edit those works. A public wiki that anybody can edit is an example of such a server. A "Massive Multiauthor Collaboration" (or "MMC") contained in the site means any set of copyrightable works thus published on the MMC site.

"CC-BY-SA" means the Creative Commons Attribution-Share Alike 3.0 license published by Creative Commons Corporation, a not-for-profit corporation with a principal place of business in San Francisco, California, as well as future copyleft versions of that license published by that same organization.

"Incorporate" means to publish or republish a Document, in whole or in part, as part of another Document.

An MMC is "eligible for relicensing" if it is licensed under this License, and if all works that were first published under this License somewhere other than this MMC, and subsequently incorporated in whole or in part into the MMC, (1) had no cover texts or invariant sections, and (2) were thus incorporated prior to November 1, 2008.

The operator of an MMC Site may republish an MMC contained in the site under CC-BY-SA on the same site at any time before August 1, 2009, provided the MMC is eligible for relicensing.

ADDENDUM: How to use this License for your documents

To use this License in a document you have written, include a copy of the License in the document and put the following copyright and license notices just after the title page:

```
Copyright (C)  year  your name.
Permission is granted to copy, distribute and/or modify this document
under the terms of the GNU Free Documentation License, Version 1.3
or any later version published by the Free Software Foundation;
with no Invariant Sections, no Front-Cover Texts, and no Back-Cover
Texts.  A copy of the license is included in the section entitled ''GNU
Free Documentation License''.
```

If you have Invariant Sections, Front-Cover Texts and Back-Cover Texts, replace the "with...Texts." line with this:

```
with the Invariant Sections being list their titles, with
the Front-Cover Texts being list, and with the Back-Cover Texts
being list.
```

If you have Invariant Sections without Cover Texts, or some other combination of the three, merge those two alternatives to suit the situation.

If your document contains nontrivial examples of program code, we recommend releasing these examples in parallel under your choice of free software license, such as the GNU General Public License, to permit their use in free software.

Function and Data Index

Concept Index